The Armenians in America

M. Vartan Malcom

The Armenians in America

Copyright © 2018 Indo-European Publishing

The present edition is a reproduction of previous publication of this work. Minor typographical errors may have been corrected without note, however, for an authentic reading experience the spelling, punctuation, and capitalization have been retained from the original text.

ISBN: 978-1-60444-928-0

CONTENTS

Author's Note iii
Preface by Leo Dominian v
Introduction by Hon. James W. Gerard viii

Chapter I
ARMENIA AND THE ARMENIANS 1

Chapter II
THE PIONEERS 33

Chapter III
IMMIGRATION AND DISTRIBUTION 40

Chapter IV
CAUSES OF IMMIGRATION 50

Chapter V
THE ARMENIANS IN INDUSTRIES 54

Chapter VI
RELIGION AND EDUCATION 67

Chapter VII
ASSOCIATIONS, PARTIES AND THE PRESS 78

Chapter VIII
CONJUGAL AND LIVING CONDITIONS 86

Chapter IX
THE FUTURE 93

AUTHOR'S NOTE

It was the lack of a handy book on the subject of the Armenians in America which first induced me to undertake the preparation of this volume. My original intention contemplated a larger edition, containing more extended historical and statistical records. But the sudden cessation of the war and the consequent rise of great national and economic questions, particularly those touching the Armenian people, have made it advisable not to wait any longer.

The primary object of this book, as indicated by its title, is to present a sketch of the history, life and activities of the Armenians in the United States. Circumstances, however, have incidentally added a greater importance to it. Those who are competent to judge and speak of the Armenians have described them as "The Anglo-Saxons of the East." They are unanimous in their belief that these people are not only one of the superior races in Southeastern Europe and Asia Minor, but by far the most fit and capable of self-government. Unfortunately it has been impossible to lay before the public concrete, unbiased and authentic facts and figures to sustain these opinions. I trust that the record of their colony in America, based principally on the official reports of the United States Government, will add weight to these assertions.

I wish to acknowledge my thanks to Hon. James W. Gerard for his Introduction to the volume and to Mr. Leon Dominian for the Preface. My thanks are also due to my classmate, Mr. Henry H. King, for reading and correcting the manuscript. I am also indebted to my friend, Mr. Royal B. Farnum, for the drawing of the cover design, and to Mrs. Malcom for her valuable assistance.

M. Vartan Malcom.
New York City, February, 1919.

PREFACE

Precious indeed is the piecing together by Mr. Malcom of the fragments of the story of Armenian immigration to the United States. Its early beginning will be a revelation to most readers. Few perhaps, among Americans of Armenian descent, were better qualified than the author to undertake the task. A lawyer by training, having acquired the ability to discern fact from fancy, he has coupled his professional experience with his knowledge of the life and social conditions among Armenians living in America. The results of his researches have a twofold value. They show first the Armenians' historical background, thereby helping to dispel many of the prevalent errors concerning this people. Moreover, they portray faithfully the manner in which the Armenians are being gradually absorbed by the population of this country.

Their immigration to these hospitable shores has been eminently free from mercenary motives. They came not at the mere beck of factory owners, like so many in the foreign throngs which crowded westbound transatlantic liners in the past twenty-five years. Rather, the outstanding fact of Armenian immigration is its analogy, in respect to motive, with the early movements of European population to our land of freedom. Almost every Armenian in the country is a refugee from persecution of the most abhorrent character, in proof of which the data culled from United States government reports by Mr. Malcom suffice when compared with the history of atrocities perpetrated on the Armenians of Turkey.

As the Puritans of old, and in truth with many similar traits of character, they came bringing the same earnestness of religious conviction, the same willingness to endure hardships of pioneer life and the same belief ingrained in their minds that they were traveling to a free land. In this last aspect the healthy seed sown by American educational endeavor in the Near East has borne good fruit. This in itself was a privilege rarely shared by immigrants from other parts of the old world.

The potential value of their racial contribution to the American strain will be found in the picture of their past. The Armenians' proper place in history has hardly yet come to light. Enough is known, however, for an appreciation of the truth that, as a people, they were strong in all those spiritual elements of true permanence and depth which alone give real strength. For at least a thousand years and probably for twice and thrice that period they have been subjected to the worst onslaughts of Asiatic barbarity. Yet their spirit never faltered and it is because of their indomitable will to defend at any price the ideals which they held in common with the peoples of the occidental world that they have survived as a distinct people.

They might have surrendered a thousand years ago, or else five centuries before this day. Had this course been theirs, the awful vision of the Asiatic sink of corruption overflowing on European soil to its westernmost shores is quickly conjured, with its foul accompaniment of eunuchs, concubines and spies. But the Armenians remained faithful wardens of Christianity's and western civilization's southeastern gates. Century in and century out they defended the mountain passes which led from Asia into Europe, holding it light to die in order that great ideals of humanity might survive. Amid doleful and corpse-strewn ruins their bitter sacrifice was consummated. For this service to civilization, for the fact that they could neither be tempted nor bribed to mingle as one with the conquering hordes of savages released by Central Asia's sandy wastes, they represent to-day the creditors of a civilized world for a debt of culture which is still unpaid.

A strain of such temper is as enviable as any in the varied racial composition of population. Analyzing this feature somewhat more deeply we find that from a strictly scientific standpoint the Armenians form part of that splendid race of mountain men-the same wherever it occurs, be it in the hills of Scotland or in the mountains of Switzerland – to mention these alone – which has always been characterized by its strong inclination for order and organization, as well as by high intellectual attainment. Thus, although having lived among Turks in Western Asia, the Armenian is related by blood far more closely to the Scotch or Swiss than to his conquerors.

Proceeding however farther away from the north than his western cousins he carries in him a glow of southern climes which, it is true, is attenuated by rocky altitude He thus combines endurance and steadfastness of purpose with a lively imagination - plainly a matchless blend for the perpetuation of high ideals. Such, to the common fund of American culture, will have been the Armenian's contribution.

As far as can be ascertained, few among the Armenians in America will return to their native land. As in the case of every well-meaning immigrant stock, the second generation is thoroughly Americanized. Descendants of the small band of early arrivals have all been assimilated beyond recognition, which is as it should be. But the pride and consciousness of American nationality need not lessen the sympathy with which they will follow the endeavors of the three or four millions over there who, after so many destructive centuries, are rising anew to the happy prospect of safeguarded development.

Leon Dominian.

Washington, D. C, February 15, 1919.

INTRODUCTION

The Armenians form one of the smaller groups of peoples that have been streaming into the United States from Southeastern Europe and the Ottoman Empire during the last twenty-five years or more. While they represent only a fraction of our large foreign population still their importance is recognized by students of American history. It is estimated that about eighty thousand of them have settled in the United States and Canada. Investigation shows that Armenians may be found in all important cities within the United States and our Dependencies overseas, but the great bulk of them are congregated in the New England States, New York, Pennsylvania, Illinois, Wisconsin, Michigan and California.

It is not generally known that there were Armenians in this country prior to the massacres of 1894, 1895 and 1896 which drove them out of their native land. Mr. Malcom's historical researches have brought out the illuminating and interesting fact that Armenians had a share in the early struggles of this Republic. The romantic adventures of "Martin the Armenian" and "George the Armenian" should lead to further research into the sources of our colonial history, because every indication points to the probability that other Armenians may have ventured to seek their fortune on this continent, and thus be among the original settlers in America.

There seems to be no doubt that most Armenians we meet in the United States to-day came here within the last twenty-five years, and this fact in itself raises an inquiry as to the reason of their immigration to this particular country. Much has been written and said concerning the thousands who have been induced to rush to America through the efforts of steamship agencies and great industrial concerns seeking cheaper labor. The Armenians happily seem to be entirely free from these influences. They emigrated in order to escape persecution from the Turks, but they chose the United States on account of their love for the American missionaries.

The record of their character, life and activities in our country brings to light the substantial qualities of the Armenian people. By comparison they stand head and shoulder above all other immigrant races from Southeastern Europe and Asia Minor, which is surprising when one considers the fact that they are geographically isolated from direct contact with modern European civilization and that they are more oppressed than any other. Over forty per cent of the Armenians admitted into the United States are, according to the classification of our Immigration Bureau, skilled laborers and educated professional men and women - a record which no other class of immigrants from that part of the world equals or even approaches. The average earnings of an Armenian laborer is greater than that of a workman of other nationalities in the same industries. There is less illiteracy among them, and in one particular locality, California, the Immigration Commission makes special mention of the fact that the average of literates among the Armenians is even higher than among the Germans. The zeal with which they have quickly and tenaciously taken advantage of the educational opportunities in America manifests intelligence, and one is astonished at the number of Armenian children in our public schools as compared with the number of children of other races. In the sphere of their home life even the ordinary workmen have better quarters than those of what are known as older immigrants. Their desire and ability to become good American citizens is surpassed by none.

Were the Armenians a weak people they would have been assimilated and lost many centuries ago. They owe their survival as a distinct nation to-day to their idealism, their courage and to the higher type of their civilization which could not be overcome and subdued by superior physical force. Their life and achievements in the United States manifest anew the strong national characteristics which have distinguished them for ages.

I cannot permit this opportunity to pass without saying that I believe the Armenians in the United States will play an important role in the regeneration and reconstruction of their country. They have here a good number of educated men and women who can become leaders of the people in Armenia. There are editors, teachers, doctors, dentists, lawyers, engineers, professors, manufacturers and merchants – ninety per cent of whom have been educated in our Colleges and Universities and who have received their practical training in the United States. These men will contribute materially to rebuilding Armenia. Dr. Barton has said: "Give the Armenian capital and a righteous government and he will turn the whole of Turkey into a Garden of Eden in ten years." I never appreciated the real significance and force of Dr. Barton's statement until I had before me this concrete analysis and comparison of the Armenian people. In this respect Mr. Malcom's book is not only a valuable addition to our current literature on the problem of immigration, but also a faithful portrait of the character and quality of the Armenian people. It contains an, inventory of what the Armenians have, not what they have lost; what they are capable of accomplishing under fair opportunities, not what they have failed to do against insurmountable obstacles.

James W. Gebaed.

New York City.

Chapter I

ARMENIA AND THE ARMENIANS

A VOLUME concerning a single race of immigrants in the United States requires by way of introduction a brief but comprehensive statement of their origin, their nationality, their language, their creed, their past and their present position among the civilized nations of the world. Such a preliminary geographical setting and historical background is especially indispensable in the case of the Armenians because they are frequently considered identical with the Turks, the Syrians, the Jews, the Persians, the Bulgarians, the Greeks or some other of the many peoples that likewise immigrate to this country from Southeastern Europe and Asia Minor.

Armenia: The historic Kingdom of Armenia lies south of the Black Sea, extending westward to the Gulf of Alexandretta on the Mediterranean, eastward to the Caspian Sea and southward to the plains of Mesopotamia. Topographically it is a high mountainous plateau. The boundaries of the country are indicated on the accompanying map by the black lines. It consists of eleven Provinces and contains about 151,893[1] square miles. The Provinces of Kars, Erivan and the eastern portion of Elizabethpol constitute what is known as Russian Armenia, and is now included in the Transcaucasian district of Russia; the Vilayet or Province of Azerbijan, known as Persian Armenia, is incorporated with Persia; and the Vilayets of Van, Bitlis, Erzerum, Diarbekir, Sivas, Mamuret-ul-Aziz, called Turkish Armenia, and Cilicia, known as Lesser Armenia, are under Turkey. Thus the whole of Armenia is divided to-day into three

---

[1] Statement Year Book, 1918.

1

parts and these divisions are designated on the map by the dotted lines.

Population: Accurate statistics of the number of Armenians in the world have never been compiled. The Ambassadorial conference at London in 1913 estimated 2,103,000 Armenians in the Ottoman Empire; 2,008,000 in the Caucasus and Russian Armenia; 165,000 in Persia and 300,000 in the United States, Canada, South America, India, Africa and Europe, – total 4,576,000. The most recent and most reliable figures are those published by the Armenian Catholicos in 1916 and the Armenian Patriarchate at Constantinople in 1912. According to these authorities the number of Armenians in Turkish Armenia was 1,018,000 and 1,082,000 in other parts of the Ottoman Empire, 1,636,486 in Russian Armenia and the Caucasus, and about 400,000 in other parts of Russia; 165,000 in Persia and 300,000 in all other countries, - total 4,601,486. It is reasonably safe to say that before the outbreak of the recent war there were at least 4,500,000 Armenians, of whom 4,000,000 lived in, and territories immediately adjacent to, their native land. But this number has been reduced by 1,000,000 through the deportations and massacres of 1915 and 1916, leaving a balance of 3,000,000 in or near Armenia, and a total of 3,500,000 in the world. There are Armenian colonies in America, England, France, Switzerland, Italy, Egypt, India, Bulgaria, Roumania, Greece, Poland, Galicia, Transylvania and Austria-Hungary.

The origin of some of these settlements dates so far back that they have practically lost their identity with the main body of the nation[2]. But on account of their existence it is said, and too often repeated, that the Armenians, like the Jews, are the most scattered race in the world. The common interpretation of this!

---

[2] See "Histoire Modern des Armeniens" by K. J. Basmadjian. For an interesting account of the Armenians in India, Bee Mesrob J. Seth's "The History of the Armenians in India." Lucas & Co., London, 1897.

statement gives an erroneous conception of the solidarity and unity of the Armenian people. It is true that there are Armenians all over the world just as there are American, English, French, German and Italian colonies in nearly every corner of the globe. Nevertheless six-sevenths of the entire Armenian population inhabit their native land – that is, out of a total of 3,500,000, at least 3,000,000 are in or near Armenia. The same cannot be said of the Jews. As a matter of fact, there are comparatively fewer Armenians living outside of their homeland than Greeks, Bulgarians, Servians, or Roumanians.

Ethnology. The fact that Armenia is geographically located in Asia Minor has given rise to the impression that its native inhabitants are Asiatics. The testimony of the world's greatest historians, philologists and anthropologists, however, proves beyond a question of doubt that the Armenians are Aryan and belong to the same racial stock as all European peoples. Just as the white man supplanted the Indian in America, so the Armenians, centuries before the Christian era, migrated from Southeastern Europe into Asia Minor and; established there the ancient State of Armenia. Homer and Herodotus refer to them as Phrygian colonists; Strabo states that they came from Thessaly; and the late Colonel Henry F. B. Lynch, the best modern authority on the subject, says: "All the evidence points to the conclusion that they (the Armenians) entered their historical seat from the west, as a branch of considerable immigration of IndoEuropean peoples crossing the straits from Europe into Asia Minor and perhaps originally coining from homes in the steppes north of the Black Sea." The Armenian language, too, in the opinion of such well-known philologists as Hubchmann and St. Martin, is IndoEuropean, and this is a strong factor in determining the racial status of the people who speak it. Moreover, the studies of ethnologists, based on the most approved scientific investigation and test, show the Armenians to be Aryan. Professor William Z. Ripley, in his notable book on "The Races of Europe," declares:

"The second racial type in this borderland (Armenia) between Europe and Asia we may safely follow Chantre in calling Armenoid, because the Armenians most clearly represent it to-day. . . . The similarity of this to our Alpine races of western Europe has been especially emphasized by the most competent authority, von Luschan. . . . Were it not for the potent selective influence of religion (Christianity and Mohammedanism), complete rupture by the invading Tatar-Turks might conceivably have taken place. As it is, the continuity of the Alpine races across Asia Minor can not be doubted."

References: Homer's Iliad II, line 862-868; Herodotus i, 72 and 194, V, 49-52, and VII, 78; "The geography of Strabo," H. C. Hamilton's translation, London, Vol. II, Page 272. Lynch's "Armenia, Travels and Studies," London, Vol. II, Page 67. This work is by far the most exhaustive, the most thorough and undoubtedly the most authoritative on the subject; Heinrich Hübschmann, "Armenische Grammatik," Leipzig, 1897; William Z. Ripley, "The Races of Europe," pages 444-448.

Strabo's reference to Armenia is as follows: "There exists an ancient account of the origin of this nation to this effect. Armenus of Armenium, a Thessalian city, which lies between Pheree and Larisa on the lake Boebe, accompanied Jason, as we have already said, in his expedition into Armenia and from Armenus the country had its name. The dress of the Armenian people is said to be of Thessalian origin. . . . The tragedians imitate the Thessalians in their attire. The passion for riding and the care of horses characterize the Thessalians and are common to Armenians."

"Like the English, the French and most other nations, the Armenians have developed a specific type of countenance. There are marked differences of pigmentation, feature and build between the Armenians of the East, West, and South and

between the mountaineers, plaindwellers and people of the towns." Treatment of the Armenians in the Ottoman Empire (1915-1916), Documents Presented to Viscount Grey of Fallodon, by Viscount Bryce; G. P. Putnam's Sons (1916), page 596.

Language, Literature and Art. The root of the Armenian language is Indo-European. The old theory that it is a branch of the Persian, with whom the Armenians have been neighbors for many centuries, has been disproved by recent scientifically conducted studies. The present Armenian alphabet, consisting of thirty-six letters, was invented by Sahag and Mesrob, in the 5th century, A. D.

The classical Armenian, like the classical Greek and Latin, is no longer in use.

What literature the Armenians possessed in ancient times was completely destroyed when the nation adopted Christianity as a state religion in the 4th century A. D. There is no doubt that they had some written literature before that because when Lucullus besieged Tigranagerta, the capital of Armenia, in 69 B. C, he found a theatre there. With the introduction of the present alphabet a translation of the Bible, described as the "Queen of Versions," was completed in 410 A. D. This was followed with a history of Armenia by Moses of Khorene. From that time up to the 17th century Armenian literature contains for the most part religious, historical and philosophical writings, in all of which it is exceedingly rich. Dulaurier, a distinguished French scholar, refers to these in glowing terms: "The glory of the Armenian literature is the abundance and preciousness of her historical records. These records, succeeding each other uninterruptedly from the beginning of the fourth century to our day, form a golden chain which connects the old world with our own. Historians describing on the one hand the heroic resistance, the courage, the selfdenial of a Christian people, on the other hand

5

the barbarity and cruelty of their victorious oppressors, form a vivid scene of tragedy."

Armenian music and Armenian art are closely associated with the Armenian Church. Besides the beautiful ecclesiastical music, there are many sad, plaintive folk-songs. In the field of art, church edifices furnish the best example of Armenian architecture and mural painting. Speaking of the ruins of Anni, another capital of Armenia where there were 1001 churches, Lynch credits the Armenians with the origin of the Gothic style. He says: "These monuments are examples of the Armenian style at its very best. . . . The merits of the style are the diversity of its resources, the elegance of the ornament in low relief, the perfect execution of every part. It combines many of the characteristics of Byzantine art and of the style which we term Gothic, and which at that date was still unborn. The conical roofs of the domes are a distinctive feature, as also are the purely Oriental niches. Texier is of opinion that the former of these features was carried into Central Europe by
the colonies of the emigrants from the city on the Arpa Chai.

"But a lesson of wider import transcending the sphere of the history of architecture, may be derived from a visit to the capital (Anni) of the Bagratid Dynasty, and from the study of the living evidence of a vanished civilization which is lavished upon the traveller within her walls. Her monuments throw a strong light upon the character of the Armenian people, and they bring into pronouncement important features of Armenian history. They leave no doubt that these people may be included in the small number of races who have shown themselves susceptible of the highest culture." The exquisite beauty of Armenian laces, mosaic work, and gold and silversmiths' handicraft are famous the world over. The late Ohanness Ayvazovsky, one of the greatest marine painters in modern times, was an Armenian. Other artists, sculptors and musicians have, won distinction in American and European capitals. The most imposing buildings in Turkey are the works of Armenian architects. Sir Edwin Pears, an English resident in Constantinople for forty years, believes the Armenian to be the most artistic and musical race in the Ottoman Empire.

References: E. Dulaurier, "Literature Armenienne," Review de L'Orient, Ser. 8, Vol. Ill, pages 95-106. "Armenia, Travels and Studies," by Henry F. B. Lynch, Vol. I, pages 890 and 891.

For Armenian Literature, see "Armenian Poems," rendered into English by Alice Stone Blackwell, Boston, 1917. "Armenian Legends and Poems," in English, beautifully illustrated, compiled by Zabelle C. Boyajian, London, 1916. This contains an introduction by Lord Bryce and an excellent essay by Aram Raffi on Armenian Epics, Folk Songs, ancient and modern poetry. "L'Armenie, son Histoire, sa Literature, son Role en l'Orient," by Archag Tchobanian, with an introduction by Anatole France, Paris, 1897. "Poemes Armemens," also by Archag Tchobanian, with an introduction by Paul Adam, Paris, 1908. "L'Orient Inedit – Legendes et Traditions Armeniennes," by Minas Tcheraz, Paris, 1912. The following contemporary publications contain translations of Armenian poems and stories, and articles of timely interest: "The New Armenia," 949 Broadway, New York City; "The Armenian Herald," Old South Building, Boston, Mass.; "Ararat," London, England; "La Voix de L'Armenie," 80 Rue Jacob, Paris; and Armenia (in Italian), Carso Reg. Margherita 78, Torino, Italy.

The following is a partial list of noted men who have studied and admired the Armenian language and literature: Lord Byron, John Brand, Sir Henry Norman, William Whiston, George Whiston, Edward Tombe, F. Conybeare, Longlois, Brosset, St. Martin, Professor Macler, Dore, Villefroi, Vetler, Newman, Miller, Peterman, Hiibschmann and others.

For Armenian Art, see the International Encyclopaedia and the references there. For Armenian Music, try on your phonograph some of the excellent records made for the Columbia Grtiphophone Co., by Mr. Shah Mouradian and Mr. Torcom Bezazian.

Religion: Before their conversion to Christianity the Armenians were Zoroastrians. They had a system of gods and customs peculiar to sun worshippers about which Professor M. H. Ananikian of the Hartford Theological Seminary has a very interesting and scholarly contribution in the Hastings' Encyclopaedia of Religion and Ethics.

The Christian religion was first introduced to the Armenians by the Apostles Thaddeus (35-43 A. D.) and Bartholomew (44-50 A. D.) . The graves of these Saints are in the monasteries at Magou and Baschkale respectively, "which lie in the western part of Armenia." In 301 A. D. King Tiridates was converted by St. Gregory the Illuminator and the Christian faith established, for the first time in the history of the world, as a state religion. It is on the basis of these historical facts that the Armenian Church is officially known as St. Gregory the Illuminator's Armenian Apostolic Church. It is often referred to under such titles as The Church of Armenia, or The Armenian Apostolic Church, or The Armenian Gregorian Church.[3]

Some of the distinctive features of The Church of Armenia deserve special mention here. In the first place it is absolutely independent of any other ecclesiastical institution in the world. It has no connection whatsoever with either the Greek or the Roman Catholic Churches, but like the latter it claims to be Apostolic. It is unique in the annals of Church history in that it

---

[3] The best authority on the Armenian Gregorian Church is Ex-Patriarch Malaohia Ormanian's book entitled "The Church of Armenia. A translation of it in English, with an introduction by Bishop Welldon of London, was published in England, 1912. See also "The Armenian Church-History, liturgy, Doctrines and Ceremonies," by E. F. Fortesoue, London, 1872.

8

was founded by an Armenian, for the Armenians and belongs to the Armenians, and in this respect it not only represents a distinct religion but the religion of a distinct people. It has never sought to proselytize other races or peoples or Individuals to its faith. Its service to the Armenians cannot be overestimated, for whatever art, literature, poetry, history and national consciousness they possess is due particularly to the influence of this great Church.

The supreme head of the Armenian church, called the Catholicos, is also the chief representative of the Armenian nation He is elected for life by the clergy and the people, and I might add here that the system of elections by popular vote has been used by the Armenians for many centuries. There are various sects of the clergy. The ordinary Parish priests are called Derders and they are permitted to marry, but once only. The Vartabeds, Bishops and the Archbishops follow in the order named. These take the vow of celibacy. The general form of worship conducted in the Armenian Church is similar to that of the Greek but its polity is like the Episcopalian. With the exception of the sermon, nearly the whole of the service is in music. In the matter of religious dogmas the Armenian Church adheres to the belief that the Holy Spirit proceeds from God only; that regeneration by baptism is possible and that there is no purgatory. Prayer to saints to intercede for the suppliant is practised. Confession is allowed, but before confessing one is required to perform certain strict penance. Over eighty per cent of the Armenian people belong to the Church of Armenia.

There are about 150,000 Roman Catholic Armenians. The Dominican Fathers as early as the 14th century and the Jesuits in the 17th century penetrated the heart of Armenia and established there their missions, some of which are still in existence. The coming of the Crusaders was also an important factor in introducing Catholicism to the Armenians in Cilicia. In 1717 one named Mekhitar of Sivas became a Catholic and subsequently founded the famous monastery which bears his name on the island of St. Lazare, near Venice. It has been said that this is one of the greatest and most picturesque institutions among the Armenians. Its library contains a fine collection of old Armenian manuscripts. It has a picture gallery containing "many works of art by Armenians which have won the approval of Ruskin."[4] The monastery also has one of the best printing establishments in Europe. A few of the most noted Armenian men of letters have been the Mekhitarist monks: Father Leo Alishan was a distinguished poet and historian. Father Arsen Pogradouni was a great linguist; he translated into the Armenian Milton's "Paradise Lost," Homer's Iliad, the works of Sophocles, and writings of Voltaire, Racine and other French authors. Father Aitenian is the author of the modern Armenian Grammar. Father Michael Chamich wrote a history of Armenia. Father Heurmeuz translated Virgil and the writings of Bernardin St. Pierre, Fenelon and others, and also wrote many beautiful religious poems.

About the year 1831 the American Board of Commissioners for Foreign Missions commenced its work among the Armenians in Turkey, as a result of which there are now probably over 150,000 Armenian Protestants. This rapid growth of Protestantism is partly due to the fact that the Protestants formed a special community under the Turkish law and on account of the presence of the American missionaries, they received greater protection from the government than the Armenian Gregorians. The endeavors of the American missionaries in Turkey are well known in America. Through the individual efforts of certain missionaries a number of schools have been founded, such as Robert College and Girls' College in Constantinople, colleges at Marsovan, Harpout, Sivas, Aintab and Beirut, which are attended by Armenians as well as Greeks, Bulgarians, Syrians and other nationalities. They have also established primary schools, churches, Bible study classes and medical stations. During the

---

[4] " Turkey and Its People, " by Sir Edwin Pears. Page 274.

massacres they have collected money from Americans and have used the same to alleviate the suffering of the natives. French, English, Swiss, Italian and German missionaries also have schools and hospitals. They, too, particularly the French and the Swiss, have rendered very valuable educational and philanthropic service to the Armenians. On the other hand the Armenians maintain their own public institutions. The Church of Armenia has thousands of parishes all over Turkish Armenia, Russian Armenia, and in other cities in the Ottoman Empire. These are centers of civic activities. In 1902 the Armenians maintained over 803 schools, with 2088 teachers and 81,226 pupils.

In so far as the Armenians are concerned the influence of the American missionaries in Turkey has been twofold. They have stimulated the Armenians to better their own educational institutions and to introduce some modern ideas and reforms in the Armenian Church. They have drawn students to American Colleges and opened America to Armenian immigration. On the other hand the introduction of Protestantism has been a severe blow to the unity of the nation because the Church of Armenia has been for centuries the fortress of the Armenian people. And again this constant appeal by the missionaries – American, French, English, German, etc. – for funds to support their institution in Turkey, has left an unpleasant impression on the public. The sympathy of audiences has been aroused by depicting the massacres perpetrated on the Armenians and the misery of these people, although Syrians, Greeks, Bulgarians and even Turks have enjoyed the benefits of missionary schools and hospitals. Thus the average man in England, in France, in the United States, has the idea that the Armenians are always begging, notwithstanding the fact that they have had nothing to do with the collection of money and are by nature averse to charity.

People think that these Christians are butchered like flocks of sheep instead of putting up a manly defense; that they have no church, no religion, no schools, and in fact nothing except what the missionaries furnish them with. Of course all these notions are absolutely incorrect. It is true that the standard of the institutions maintained by the Armenians do not come up to similar institutions in France, England and America, but it must not be forgotten that what the Armenians are as a nation and what they have as a nation is far above the standard and quality of any other race in the Balkans and the Near East.

I cannot close this subject without referring to another topic. One often hears that the Armenians are individualistic and disunited. I disagree. I believe the Armenians are more united than most other races. What nation is there whose population has been divided against its will into three parts and each part ruled over by sovereigns hostile to each other and hostile to the natives, and yet in every crisis of national existence that subject race has held together tenaciously? What seems to be disunion and individualism among the Armenians is only skin deep and due to two things. One, the division of their country between Russia, Turkey and Persia; the other, the diverse training of their leaders. Some Armenians are educated in the Armenian national schools, some in American missionary institutions, some under the care of the Jesuits and others under the care of the Mekhitarists; some go to Italy, others to France, and still others to Russia or to England or the United States for their education. When these men get together there is no cohesion of ideas and aims. Thus, while missionary effort of every kind is appreciated by the Armenians, on the other hand they realize the mischief it has unconsciously caused to the nation. Hence it is the earnest hope of every thinking Armenian that when their country regains its independence, the zeal of the missionaries will be subservient to the measures that must be enforced in order to guard the unity of the nation and to establish a common ground for the training of the coming generation.

History: It is beyond the scope of this chapter to attempt even a bare outline of the history of the Armenian people, which extends back to remote antiquity. Suffice it to say on the authority of the existing records that the Armenians have lived in Armenia and have been in possession of their native land for over 2,500 years. During all these centuries their country has been subject to many invasions both from the east and from the west, because it is the direct highway between Asia and Europe. Their history is connected with the history of Persia, Greece, Rome and the Byzantine Empire. Their early adoption of Christianity, their distinct language, and the rugged mountainous character of their country have been vital factors in developing a strong nationality which has survived down to this day. The inestimable services this little isolated Christian country has rendered to mankind are often forgotten. Armenia has been for ages the frontier of our civilization. If it were not for it, the people we call Turks would have destroyed the Byzantine Empire hundreds of years before the 14th century and would have overrun Europe at a time when none of the present nations were strong enough to turn them back as they did at the gates of union and individualism among the I is only skin deep and due to two t the division of their country between Turkey and Persia; the other, the divei ing of their leaders. Some Armenian educated in the Armenian national some in American missionary some under the care of the Jesuits t under the care of the Mekhitarists; s Italy, others to France, and still othersia or to England or the United State education. When these men get togeti is no cohesion of ideas and aims. Thus, while missionary effort of every kind is appreciated by the Armenians, on the other hand they realize the mischief it has unconsciou to the nation. Hence it is the earnest every thinking Armenian that I country regains its independence, the zeal of the missionaries will be subservient measures that must be enforced in guard the unity of the nation and to i common ground for the training of the generation.

History: It is beyond the scope of this chapter to attempt even a bare outline of Vienna in 1688. It is an historical fact that the Armenian people saved modern civilization by delaying the Tartar-Turks of Asia from invading Europe earlier than they did.

Armenian dynasties: Arsacid 149 B. C. to 428 A. D., Bagratid 478 A. D. to 1079 A. D., Ardzrunian 908 A. D. to 1080 A. D., Rupenian 1080-1898.

Armenian Emperors and Empresses of the Byzantine Empire; Maurice (582-601), Philip (711-718), Leo (818-820), Basil (867-886), Leo (886-912), Alexander (912-918), Constantin (918-920), Romanos (920-944), Romanos II (989-968), John (969-976), Basil II (9761025), and Constantin II (1025-1028); Empresses: Marianna (788), Theodora (818-820), Euprosina (828), Theodora I (880), Heghine (919), Theodora II (971), Theodora III (1042) and Rita (1296).

Other illustrious Armenians. According to P. J. Aucher, an Armenian named Narsas (542-568) was Emperor Justinian's great general and a favorite of Theodora. Another Armenian by the name of Isaac, says the same historian, "held the destiny of all Italy in his hand as the Exarch of Ravenna." (625-648.) Prince Pakradon, an Armenian, fought Napoleon at Moscow. Loris Melikoff, another Armenian, was the Commander-in-Chief of the Russian army in the Caucasus in the war of 1877 and the personal advisor of Alexander II of Russia. Prince Malcolm Khan has rendered great service to Persia. Nubar Pasha, twice the Prime Minister of Egypt, and Lucasz, Prime Minister of Hungary in 1918, were also Armenians. Armenians who have held high administrative offices in the government of Turkey are too numerous to mention here. Most of the treasurers of the Sultans have been Armenians.

When the Turks finally took Constantinople in 1453 they had already conquered the whole of Asia Minor, and Armenia, Arabia, Syria, Palestine and Mesopotamia had passed into their hands. They now pushed their conquests westward in Europe and before long added Greece, Servia, Bulgaria, Roumania, Albania, Macedonia, Montenegro, Herzegovina and Bosnia to the possessions. Favored by the diversity of nationalities, languages, interest and geographical barriers, the Sultans were able to keep the native inhabitants of these countries subdued by brute military force. They imposed on them a crude form of government. First: The non-Moslem population of this new Mohammedan Empire were divided into communities, called "Millets," on the basis of either language or religion, and each millet was granted the right to maintain, under certain strict restrictions and at its own expense, schools, churches, hospitals, newspapers and other institutions of a local character. The adoption of this system was absolutely necessary because fusion was impossible between the Turks and the Christian subjects. Under this system the Armenians were subdivided into three distinct millets, viz., the "Ermeni Millet," composed of those who belonged to the Church of Armenia; the "Katholik Millet," composed of those who belonged to the Roman Catholic Church, and the "Protestant Millet," which was formed upon the request of the American missionaries and which further broke up the unity of the nation. Second: The Christians were heavily taxed and anyone who refused or was unable to pay these taxes for any reason was thereby liable to forfeit all his possessions. Bribery, blackmail and corruption of every description became common. Third: The Christians received no police protection. Brigands, thieves, soldiers, tribal chieftains would rob the peasants and the shopkeepers in the villages, would carry away their flocks and goods, would commit murder and rape, and all go unpunished. The Christians were excluded from the army and forbidden under penalty of death to carry arms of any kind and therefore had no means of defense against these outrages. Fourth: The administration of justice was so deplorable that all European powers maintained their own consular courts for the protection of their own citizens. But the natives were necessarily obliged to resort to Ottoman courts where the testimony of a Christian was inadmissible against a Moslem, and consequently no judgment or satisfaction could be obtained. ExPresident William Howard Taft, in a public address delivered in Brooklyn, N. Y., on January 10, 1918, very correctly sums up the character of the Ottoman Government in these words: "It is a lawless form of medieval autocracy imposed on subject races by pressure from without; sustained by fraud and force; knowing no law; despising justice; alien to every instinct of humanity; deaf to sympathy and glorying in the shame of the power to injure and destroy."

The first to rebel against these oppressors were the Greeks (1821), who with the help of England, France and Russia succeeded in regaining their independence (1832). Next Servia and Montenegro arose against the Sultan, and Bulgaria followed suit. In order to check these revolutionary movements of his subject peoples, the Sultan instigated the Bulgarian massacres. Thereupon, for the avowed purpose of protecting the Christians, Russia declared war (1877) on Turkey, which terminated by the signing of the Treaty of San Stefano on March 3, 1878. Article 16 of that treaty contained the following provisions:

"As the evacuation by the Russian Troops of the Territory which they occupy in Armenia, and which is to be restored to Turkey, might give rise to conflicts and complications detrimental to the maintenance of good relations between the two countries, the Sublime Porte engages to carry into effect, without further delay, the improvements and reforms demanded by local requirements in the provinces inhabited by the Armenians, and to guarantee their security from Kurds and Circassians."

16

When this treaty was signed Russian troops led by Armenian generals and composed of many Armenian soldiers, occupied a large part of the Armenian provinces referred to and thereby guaranteed protection to the Armenian inhabitants. But in order to undermine the growing power of Russia in the East, England, on June 4, 1878, entered into the following alliance with the Sultan, which is known as The Cyprus Convention.

"If Batoum, Ardahan, Kars, or any of them shall be retained by Russia, and if any attempt shall be made at any future time by Russia to take possession of any further territory of His Imperial Majesty, the Sultan, in Asia, as fixed by the definitive Treaty of Peace, England engages to join His Imperial Majesty, the Sultan, in defending them by force of arms.

"In return, His Imperial Majesty, the Sultan, promises to England to introduce necessary reforms, to be agreed upon later between the two powers, into the Government and for the protection of the Christian and other subjects of the Porte in these territories; and in order to enable England to make necessary provisions for executing her engagements, His Imperial Majesty, the Sultan, further consents to assign the Island of Cyprus to be occupied and administered by England."

It will be noticed that under this contract the consideration on the part of England is a promise to defend by force of arms the territories of Turkey, particularly those occupied by Russia under the Treaty of San Stefano, and on the part of Turkey the cession of the Island of Cyprus to Great Britain. References to the Christians is only to give the alliance an air of magnanimity and to draw the Armenians away from Russia. Needless to say that England still occupies the Island of Cyprus, while many massacres have taken place under the eyes of the English consuls.

Great Britain regarded the provisions of the Treaty of San Stefano as too severe on Turkey and forced Russia to a Congress of Powers, which on July 13, 1878, substituted in its place the Treaty of Berlin. Under this treaty, Roumania, Servia and Montenegro were declared independent. Bulgaria was made a vassal state; Bosnia and Herzegovina were put under the care of Austria-Hungary. But in order to appease the Sultan, Armenia was deliberately turned back to him under Article 61.

"The Sublime Porte undertakes to carry out, without further delay, the improvements and reforms demanded by local requirements in the provinces inhabited by Armenians, and to guarantee their security against the Circassians and Kurds. It will periodically make known the steps taken to this effect to the Powers, who will superintend their application."

What occurred since the Treaty of Berlin is singularly well described by Mr. Morgenthau, on page 288 of his recent book: "And now, as Abdul Hamid, in 1878, surveyed his shattered domain, he saw that its most dangerous spot was Armenia. He believed, rightly or wrongly, that these Armenians, like the Roumanians, the Bulgarians, the Greeks, and the Serbians, aspired to restore their independent medieval nation, and he knew that Europe and America sympathized with this ambition. The Treaty of Berlin, which had definitely ended the Turco-Russian War, contained an article which gave the European Powers a protecting hand over the Armenians. How could the Sultan free himself permanently from this danger? An enlightened administration, which would have transformed the Armenians into free men and made them safe in their lives and property and civil and religious rights, would probably have made them peaceful and loyal subjects. But the Sultan could not rise to such a conception of statesmanship as this. Instead, Abdul Hamid apparently thought that there was only one way of ridding Turkey of the Armenian problem – and that was to rid her of the Armenians. The physical destruction of 2,000,000 men, women, and children by massacres, organized and directed by the state, seems to be the one sure way of forestalling the further disruption of the Turkish Empire."

It was this idea which found expression in the terrible massacres of 1894-1896. It was the same idea which the Turks, with the help of Germany, put into execution in 1915 on a vaster and more systematically planned scale, doing away with over a million souls.

The important role the Armenians have played in the recent war has not been brought to the attention of the public because of the distance of the scene of operation. Dr. G. Pasdermadjian[5], the diplomatic representative at Washington of his Holiness the Catholicos, gives the following summary of the service his countrymen have rendered:

"In 1914 both Turkey and Russia appealed to the Armenians by various promises of a future autonomous Armenia to secure their assistance in their respective military operations. Through their long and bitter experience the Armenians knew very well that the imperialistic governments of both Turkey and of Russia were opposed to their national aspirations and therefore those promises had no value whatever. But, realizing the universal significance of the present war, and considering the fact that justice was on the side of the Entente, the Armenians, in spite of their distrust of the Russian government, from the very beginning, unreservedly bound themselves to the allied cause.

"This decision of the Armenians cost them the sacrifice of more than 1,000,000 men in Turkish Armenia, and complete devastation of their native land even in the first year of the war.

"In spite of this terrible blow, the Armenians did not lose their vigor, and, even though the autocratic Russian government, up to

---

[5] In his "Why Armenia Should Be Free." Published by the Hairenik Publishing Company, Boston, 1919.

the time of the Revolution, created all sorts of obstacles to impede their activities, they still continued their assistance to the allied cause. In bringing about the failure of the three Turkish offensives in 1914 and 1915 the Armenians gave the allied cause important armed assistance, on both sides of the TurcoRussian frontier.

"After the Russian Revolution, when the Russian military forces fled from the Caucasian front and left it unprotected from January, 1918, to the middle of the following September, the Armenians were the only people who resisted and delayed the Turco-German advance toward Baku. Moreover, the Armenians accomplished all this with their own forces, all alone, surrounded by hostile elements, without any means of communication with their great Allies of the West. As an evidence of this we may mention the fact that during the last eight months and a half the Armenians have received from the Allies only 6,500,000 rubles ($8,250,000) of financial assistance, and the 2,800 British soldiers who were too few and arrived too late to save Baku."

Lord Robert Cecil, the British under-secretary of State for Foreign Affairs, in a letter to Viscount Bryce dated September, 1918, enumerates Armenia's part in the war in the following manner:

"One: In the autumn of 1914, the national congress of the Ottoman Armenians, then sitting at Erzerum, was offered autonomy by the Turkish emissaries, if it would actively assist Turkey in the war, but it replied that while they would do their duty individually as Ottoman subjects, they could not, as a nation, work for the cause of Turkey and her allies.

"Two: Following this courageous refusal, the Ottoman Armenians were systematically murdered by the Turkish Government, in 1915 more than 700,000 people being exterminated by the most cold-blooded and fiendish methods.

"Three: From the beginning of the war, that half of the Armenian nation under Russian sovereignty organized volunteer forces and, under their heroic leader, General Andranig, bore the brunt of some of the heaviest fighting in the Caucasian campaign.

"Four: After the Russian Army's breakdown at the end of last year, these Armenian forces took over the Caucasian front and for five months delayed the Turks' advance, thus rendering important services to the British Army in Mesopotamia, these operations in the Alexandropol and Erivan region being, of course, unconnected with those of Baku.

"Armenian soldiers are still fighting in the ranks of the Allied forces in Syria (8,000 volunteers, principally from America). They are to be found serving alike in the British, the French, and in the American armies, and have borne their part in General Allenby's great victory in Palestine."

The Armenians claim the absolute independence of their country on the ground that they are lawfully entitled to sovereign possession of their native land just as much as Frenchmen are to France and Englishmen are to England; and all they ask for is their own country. Moreover, the Allies have under various treaties, not only recognized the justice of her claim but also promised to liberate her from Turkey, although they failed to carry out these solemn covenants. Furthermore, in the beginning of the recent war, the Armenians found themselves between Russia and Turkey, but they bravely joined the side of right and justice and fought as co-belligerents with the Allies. They thus sacrificed over 25 per cent of their entire population while the losses of France are said to be less than 5 or 6 per cent. No nation on either side of the war, including Belgium, Servia and Roumania, has suffered more, contributed more and shed more blood for freedom than the Armenians. And they are to-day demanding that the Great Powers shall not again make a pawn of their country, but restore it to its lawful owners and declare its complete Independence in the forthcoming Treaty[6].

Foreign Opinion on the Armenians
"The Armenians are a noble race."

DR. CYRUS HAMLIN,

Thirty -five years a missionary in Constantinople and the founder of Robert College. From a letter to the New York Herald, Dec. 18, 1894.
"To serve Armenia is to serve civilization."

W. E. GLADSTONE.

"The more we fathom their distant past, the more we begin to realize the constructive and enlightening role played by the Armenians in the world history of civilization."

HERR HAUPT

---

[6] A good modern history of Armenia is yet to be written but there are excellent passages on the subject in Lynch 's Armenia, Travels and Studies." See also History of Armenia," by Michael Chamich. On the Armenian Question, see " The Rdle of the Turk, " by Frederick D. Green, New York. 1896; " Turkey and the Armenian Atrocities," by E. M. Bliss; " Turkey and Its People," by Sir Edwin Pears; "England's Responsibility Toward Armenia, by Malcolm McCall, London; " Our Responsibility for Turkey," by the Duke of Argyll, London, 1896; "Travels and Politics in Armenia," by Noel E. Buxton, 1914. On the present war "Ambassador Morgenthau's Story," by Henry Morgenthau, New York, 1918; "Treatment of the Armenians in the Ottoman Empire" (1915-1916); Documents Presented to Viscount Grey of Fallodon, by Viscount Bryce, London, 1916; "The Pan-German Plot Unmasked," by Andre Cheradame with an introduction by Lord Cromer, London, 1917; "Two War Years in Constantinople," by Harry Stuermer, German War Correspondent, translated from the German by E. Allen, New York, 1917; "Armenia and the War," by H. P. Hacobian, with preface by Viscount Bryce, London, 1918.

A noted scholar in his "Armenia's Past and Present."

"The importance of the Armenian people is often ignored. The Armenians have played in antiquity, and more especially in the Middle Ages, an important role. As a factor of civilization in the Orient, the Armenian is more important than is generally realized. The Armenians are, without doubt, intellectually the most awake amongst all the peoples that inhabit the Ottoman Empire. They are superior to Turks and Kurds."

Professor KARL ROTH,

In his "Armenien und Deutschland."

"The Armenians constitute the sole civilizing, the sole humanizing element in Anatolia; peaceful to the degree of self-sacrifice; lawabiding to their own undoing and industrious and hopeful under conditions which would appall the majority of mankind. At their best they are the stuff of which heroes and martyrs are moulded."

Dr. E. J. DILLON

A well-known English writer on the Near East, in his "Armenia, an Appeal" Contemporary Review, 1896, Vol.69, page 1.

"The Armenians are a people of large and noble capacities. For ages they have maintained their civilization under oppression that would have crushed almost any other people. The Armenian is one of the finest races in the world. If I were asked to name the most desirable races to be added by immigration to the American population, I would name among the very first the Armenian."

The late ANDREW D. WHITE,

United States Ambassador to Germany, and founder of Cornell University, in his Autobiography.

————————

"It would be difficult to find in the annals of a nation less crime than in those of the Armenians, whose virtues are those of peace and whose vices are the result of the oppression they have undergone."

LOBD BYBON

Who studied Armenian with the Mikhitarist Father on the Island of St. Lazare.

————————

"They have all the solidity of the Turk, without his immobility; they have the quickness of perception and acuteness of the Greek, without his frivolity. In one word, they are the AngloSaxons of the East."

REV. H. O. DWIGHT

One of the first American Missionaries in Turkey, in his "Christianity in Turkey"

————————

"Among all those who dwell in western Asia they (the Armenians) stand first, with a capacity for intellectual and moral progress, as well as with a natural tenacity of will and purpose beyond that of all their neighbors— not merely of Turks, Tartars, Kurds, and Persians, but also of Russians. They are a strong race, not only with vigorous nerves and sinews, physically active and energetic, but also of conspicuous brain power."

LORD BEYCE

Ex-Ambassador of Great Britain to the United States.

"The Armenians, industrious, sober, and zealous, occupied principally with agriculture, with raising cattle, and with manufacturing carpets . . . can be considered the possessors of the highest civilization in Asia Minor. Thanks to their aptitude and their intelligence, the Armenians . . . occupy the highest positions in Turkey."

V. ROSEN

A German authority, in the Tägliche Rundschau.

———————

"We may say without exaggeration that not only in Armenia proper, but far beyond its boundaries, the economic life of Turkey rests, in great part, upon the Armenians."

DR. PAUL ROHRBACH

Another well-known German scholar.

———————

"The Syrians, in spite of their ability, have so far never been able to push beyond places of secondary, though considerable, importance. Armenians, on the other hand, have attained the highest administrative ranks, and have at times exercised a decisive influence on the conduct of public affairs in Egypt."

Lord CROMER

In his "Modern Egypt" Vol II, page 220.

"In some respects the Armenians are the most interesting

people in Asia Minor. They are physically a fine race.... It is prolific and comparatively free from the deadly maladies of immorality which, unless checked, will exterminate the Turkish race."

· ·

"I believe the Armenian race to be the most artistic in Turkey. Many paint well and some have made a reputation in Russia and France.

... I can only judge of the Armenian love for music from the fact that nearly every family which can afford a piano has one...

Every observer notes that our best native companies of actors are Armenians."

SIR EDWIN PEAKS

For forty years a distinguished member of the European Bar at Constantinople, in his "Turkey and Its People", pages 270-274.

————————

The Armenians are "physically of good stature, strong features and manly bearing; industrious and frugal; loyal to their religion and their nation; of marked ability for adapting themselves to any circumstances, whether of climate, social or political life; very kindly, sympathetic, affectionate, with an element of the jovial in their life; intensely proud of their history and their faith; clannish almost to the last degree, refusing such association with other races as might imply the loss of their own; of exceptionally pure morals among the Eastern races; intense lovers of home and family life, and hospitable in the last degree; with acute minds and suave manners, they manifest many of the essential elements of a strong nation."

EDWIN M. BLIN

Of Beirut College, in his "Turkey and the Armenian Atrocities" page US.

———————

"In the modern intellectual revival in Turkey the Armenians were the first to respond. They not only eagerly fostered modern education among themselves and in their own country, but thousands of bright Armenian young men and women have studied in the educational centers of the world and have won distinction by the superiority of their intellect and their unconquerable desire and zeal for education. There is no race on the face of the earth more worthy, by its inheritance, its intrinsic worth, its intellectual capacity and ability, its traditional industry, its peaceful temper and spirit, its domestic hopes and purposes, of a free and independent existence. In no commercial enterprise, no form of industry, no profession, and in no institution of learning in Turkey or elsewhere do the Armenians take second place.

"It was at this race that the blow of destruction was primarily aimed by the government of the Young Turks in the winter of 1914 and the spring of 1915. This historic, educated and refined people were maltreated in a thousand forms, starved and exiled. Its greatest crime is that, in contact with its Turkish neighbors, it has far outstretched all the rest in enterprise and industry; and in religion it has stood firmly against the persecution of its Mohammedan over-lords, refusing to exchange Jesus Christ for Mohammed."

(In the World Court, October, 1918.)

"I know the Armenians to be by inheritance religious, industrious and faithful. They are the Anglo-Saxons of Eastern Turkey. They are not inferior in mental ability to any race on earth. I say this after eight years' connection with Euphrates College, which has continually from 550 to 600 Armenians upon its list of students, and after superintending schools which have 4,000 more of them."

"Give the Armenian capital and a righteous government, and he will turn the whole of Turkey into a Garden of Eden in ten years."

DR. JAMES L. BARTON

The well-known Secretary of the American Board of Commissioners for Foreign Missions.

"In the Armenians we have a people who are peculiarly adapted to be the intermediaries of the new dispensation. They profess our religion, are familiar with some of our best ideals, and assimilate each new product of European culture with an avidity and thoroughness which no other race between India and the Mediterranean has given any evidence of being able to rival. These capacities they have made manifest under the greatest of disadvantages, as a subject race ministering to the needs of Mussulman masters. They know well that with every advance of true civilization they are sure to rise, as they will certainly fall at each relapse.

"The fact that in Turkey they are vigorously precluded from bearing arms has disposed superficial observers to regard them as cowards. A different judgment might be meted out were they placed on an equality in this respect with their enemies the Kurds. At all events, when given the chance, they have not been slow to display martial qualities both in the domain of the highest strategy and in that of personal prowess. The victorious commander-in-chief for Russia in her Asiatic campaign of 1877 was an Armenian from the district of Lori-Loris Melikoff. In the same campaign the most brilliant general of division in the Russian army was an Armenian – Tergukasoff. The gallant young staff-officer, Tarnaieff, who planned and led the hairbrained

28

attack on the Azizi Fort in front of Erzerum, was an Armenian, and paid for his daring with his life. At the present day the frontier police, engaged in controlling the Kurds of the border, are recruited from among Armenians. These examples may be sufficient to nail to the counter an inveterate lie, from which the Armenians have suffered, at least in British estimation, more, perhaps, than from any other supposed defects.

"If I were asked what characteristics distinguished the Armenians from other Orientals, I should be disposed to lay most stress on a quality known in popular speech as grit. It is this quality to which they owe their preservation as a people and they are not surpassed in this respect by any European nation. Their intellectual capacities are supported by a solid foundation of character, and, unlike the Greeks, but like the Germans, their nature is averse to superficial methods; they become absorbed in their tasks and plumb them deep. There is no race in the Nearer East more quick of learning than the Persians; yet should you be visited by a Persian gentleman accompanied by his Armenian man of business, take a book down from your shelves, better one with illustrations, and the conversation turning upon some subject treated by its author, hand it to them after a passing reference. The Persian will look at the pictures, which he will praise. The Armenian will devour the book and at each pause in the conversation you will see him poring over it with knitted brows. These tendencies are naturally accompanied by forethought and balance; and they have given the Armenian his pre-eminence in commercial affairs. He is not less clever than the Greek; but he sees further, and, although ingrained with the petty vices of all Oriental traders, the Armenian merchant is quick to appreciate the advantages of fair dealing when they are suggested by the conditions under which his vocation is pursued. A friend with a large experience of the Balkans, with their heterogeneous urban populations, has told me, as an interesting fact, that in the statistics of bankruptcy for those countries the proportion of the Armenians implicated is comparatively low. Inasmuch as such bankruptcies are usually more or less of a fraudulent nature, the fact indicates not, perhaps, so much the greater integrity of Armenians, as their power to resist an immediate temptation and their promptitude in recognizing the monetary value of commercial stability.

"But in order to estimate this people at anything like their true worth, one should study them not in the Levant, with its widespread corruption, but in the Russian provinces of Armenia. ... For what was it that I saw? In every trade and in every profession, in business and in the Government services the Armenian was without a rival and in full possession of the field. He equips the postal service by which you travel, and if you are so fortunate as to find an inn the landlord will be an Armenian. Most of the villages in which you sojourn are inhabited by a brawny Armenian peasantry. In the towns, if the local governor attaches to your service the head of the local police, it will be a stalwart Armenian in Russian uniform who will find you either a lodging or a shady garden in which to erect your tents. If you remark on the way some well-built edifice which aspires to architectural design, it will be the work of an Armenian builder from Alexandropol. In that city itself, where the Armenians are most numerous, the love of building, which was so marked a characteristic of their forefathers, has blossomed again among kinder circumstances; a spacious cathedral and several large churches stand among new stone houses fronted with ambitious fa9ades.... The monetary transactions of the country are in the hands of Armenian bankers. The skilled workmen – jewellers, watchmakers, carpenters – are Armenians.... Indeed were it not for the fact that the governors and chief police officials of large districts are Russians, and that Cossacks and Russian regular soldiers may here and there be seen, the traveler would not suspect that he was in a Russian province, and would go the way he listed with the most serene composure until he was rudely awakened by some abrupt collision with the Russian system and brought to his proper mind. As it is, the Armenian has edged out the Russian, and, if peace were allowed her conquests unhindered, he would ultimately rule in the land."

COL. HENRY F. B. LYNCH

In his "Armenia, Travels and Studies," Vol. I, page 466.

———————

"The Armenians of the present day are the direct descendants of the people who inhabited the country three thousand years ago. Their origin is so ancient that it is lost in fable and mystery. There are still undeciphered cuneiform inscriptions on the rocky hills of Van, the largest Armenian city, that have led certain scholars – though not many, I must admit – to identify the Armenian race with the Hittites of the Bible. What is definitely known about the Armenians, however, is that for ages they have constituted the most civilized and most industrious race in the eastern section of the Ottoman Empire. From their mountains they have spread over the Sultan's dominions, and form a considerable element in the population of all the large cities. Everywhere they are known for their industry, their intelligence, and their decent and orderly lives. They are so superior to the Turks intellectually and morally that much of the business and industry has passed into their hands. With the Greeks, the Armenians constitute the economic strength of the empire. These people became Christians in the fourth century and established the Armenian Church as their state religion. This is said to be the oldest Christian Church in existence.

"In face of persecutions which have had no parallel elsewhere these people have clung to their early Christian faith with the utmost tenacity. For fifteen hundred years they have lived there in Armenia, a little island of Christians surrounded by backward peoples of hostile religion and hostile race. Their long existence has been one unending martyrdom. The territory which they inhabit forms the connecting link between Europe and Asia, and all the Asiatic invasions – Saracens, Tartars, Mongols, Kurds and Turks – have passed over their peaceful country. For centuries they have thus been the Belgium of the East. Through all this period the Armenians have regarded themselves not as Asiatic, but as Europeans. They speak an Indo-European language, their racial origin is believed by scholars to be Aryan, and the fact that their religion is the religion of Europe has always made them turn their eyes westward. And out of that western country, they have always hoped, would some day come the deliverance that would rescue them from their murderous masters[7]."

HENRY MORGENTHAU,

Ex-United States Ambassador to Turkey, in his "Ambassador Morgenthau's Story" pages 287-9.

---

[7] For the quotations from German authors I am indebted to Mr. Arshag Mahdesian, the Editor of "The New Armenia."

Chapter II

THE PIONEERS
(1618-1894)

THERE were Armenians among the first settlers in America. We are indebted to the records of the Virginia Company of London for the interesting information that "Martin the Armenian[8]" was a member of the Colony at Jamestown, Virginia, as early as 1618 or 1619. The exact date of his landing, the name of the vessel that brought him here and the circumstances that induced him to cross the Atlantic are unknown. But all the bits of references to him put together lead to the conclusion that he came here as one of the servants of Governor George Yeardley[9]. While in Virginia he acquired British citizenship which undoubtedly entitles him to the distinction of being the first naturalized person on the American continent. After remaining here for about four years he returned to England in 1622 with a

---

[8] Bancroft Papers, Virginia (New York Public Library) , Vol. II, pages 197-199. He is probably the John Martin listed as one of the Adventurers in the Company's Book. See Force's Tracts, Vol. Ill, pamphlet called " A Declaration of the State of the Colonie and Affaires in Virginia; with the Names of the Adventurors."

[9] On September 25, 1629, Edmund Rossingham, a nephew of Governor George Yeardley, filed a claim against the latter's estate for services rendered. It appears that Yeardley had employed Rossingham in 1618 as his agent to look after his plantation in Virginia. The Privy Council referred the matter to Sir Dudley Digges, Sir Maurice Abbott and Messrs. Thomas Gibbes and Samuel Wrote. The Referees report and findings state: "and also the testimony of John Martin, servant to said George Yeardley, and then resident in Virginia, testifying the petitioner then to have had fower neate beaste" etc., Certificate of Thomas Gibbs and Samuel Wrote. British State Papers, Colonial, Vol.V, No. 15, 1, page 98.

"parcell of tobacco" which he had raised in Virginia. Upon his reaching London the customs officers imposed double the amount of the regular duties on his importation because he was a foreigner by birth. Thereupon Martin appealed to the Company's Court for a reassessment. His petition, dated May 8, 1622, reads as follows[10]:

"John Martin the Persian makinge humble suite for the Companies fauor to the ffarmors of his Mats Custome to free him from payinge double Custome wch they required of him beinge a Stranger notwithstandinge he was made a freeman in Virginia by Sr. Geo: Yeardley then Gouernor as by Certificate vnder the Collonies Seale appeared Answeare was made touchinge his freedom that none but the Kinge could makc him a free denizon of England, and for the Custome -demaunded the ffarmors themselues could not nowe remitt in reguard they had already entred the parcell into their booke and charged it vpon Account, wherevpon it beinge taken into consideration howe he might be releiued, he was at length aduised to peticon vnto my Lo: Trear for remittinge the said imposicon in reguard he was a freman of Virginia and intended to returne thither againe 1th some servante out of the proceed of that smale parcell of Tobacco he [here] brought ouer to supplie his wante."

On May 20, 1622, the Court, which was presided over by Lord Cavendish, rendered the following decision:

"The Courte takinge into consideration the request of Mr. Martin the Persian touching the double charge imposed vpon his Tobacco By the ffearmors in reguard he was a Stranger and havinge informed themselues of the priuiledge of their Patent, that giues them power to enfranchies Strangers and make them capeable thereby of the like imunities that themselues enjoy: Haue therefore ordered that the Secretary shall rep aire to the

---

[10] In the beginning of the 17th century a large part of Armenia was invaded by Shah Abas of Persia. Legally speaking Martin must have been a Persian subject.

ffarmors of the Custome with a Coppie of the said clause and that with the Courte speciall comendacon of Mr. Martin ynto them, and to entreat their fauor towarde him rather in respect of his good likinge to the Plantation whither he intends to goe againe, wch may happily encourage other strangers to the like resolucon to go ouer thither[11]."

The valuable records of the Virginia Company of London contain a number of references to this Armenian. It appears that he became a member of the Company's Standing Committee and attended many of its important sessions. He is mentioned in the minutes of an "extraordinary" meeting held on October 20, 1623, as "Martin an Armeanean." When the question as to whether or not the Company should surrender its charter to the King was put to vote, "Martin the Armenian," with Lord Argall and seven others, raised, his hand for the affirmative. "Martin Armenean" was present at an important deliberation of the Committee held on November 12, 1623. He is again referred to as "Martin ye Armenia" in another meeting that took place on January 14, 1624[12].

The next two Armenians came to America in 1653 under the most interesting circumstances. There was at this time a great deal of enthusiasm to produce silk in Virginia. Unsuccessful experiments had been made in the care and raising of silkworms and mulberry trees which furnish the chief nourishment for these caterpillars. Edward Digges, one of the leading members of the

---

[11] The Records of the Virginia Company of London. The Court Book. Edited by Susan Myra Kingsbury, Vol. I, page 633, Vol. II, page 13.

[12] Bancroft Papers, Virginia, (New York Public Library), Vol. II, pages 197-199. The Records of the Virginia Company of London; the Court Book. Edited by Susan Myra Kingsbury t Vol. II, pages 473, 477 and 498. See also British State Papers, Colonial, Vol. II, page 53. Alexander Brown, in his " The First Republic in America," page 554, suggests that the real name of Martin might have been Martian, which has all the elements and sound of a .good Armenian name. The Armenian of John is Hovanness.

Colony, having heard through his father, then the English Ambassador to Russia, that the Armenians were expert cultivators of silkworms, brought over at his own expense two of them "who enjoyed a high reputation in their native land for their skill and experience[13]." 6 The result of the work of these men was so promising that in 1654, John Ferrer, an earnest supporter of the Company, wrote a poem dedicated "To the Most Noble Deserving Esquire Digges: Upon the Arrival of His Two Armenians out of Turkey into Virginia." A part of the poem reads as follows[14]:

"But noble Diggs carries the Bell away
(Lass ! want of eggs made so small the essay)
His two Armenians from Turkey sent
Are now most busy on his bravc attempt.
And had he stock sufficient for next yeare
Ten thousand pounds of Silk would then appeare
And to the skies his worthy deeds upreare.

• •

Courage, brave Sir: Sith Ayde from God is sent
Proceed, go on, drive forth thy great intent."

In December, 1656, the Assembly of Virginia passed the following Resolution:

"That George the Armenian for his encouragement in the trade of silk and to stay in the country to follow the same have four thousand pounds of tobacco allowed him by the Assembly[15]."

It cannot be ascertained whether "George" was one of the Armenians brought over by Digges, but the evidence seems to be in favor of that presumption.

---

[13] "Economic History of Virginia in the 17th Century," by Philip A. Bruce, Vol. I, page 365.
[14] Force's Historical Tracts: Pamphlet called the "Reformed Virginia Silk-Worm/' Vol. Ill, pages 34-35.
[15] Henning's Statutes, Vol. I, page 425.

History is silent concerning other Armenians who may have drifted to the New World in quest of prosperity during the rest of the 17th and 18th centuries It is not at all improbable that through the influence of the Armenians already in Virginia others may have come here, particularly from Holland[16] and India where Armenian merchants were constantly in touch with England.

The Armenian pioneer immigrants began to come to the United States about three years after the American missionaries planted (1831) at Bebek, a suburb of Constantinople, the nucleus of their present great enterprise in the Ottoman Empire. According to the best accounts, it was Khachadoor Osgangan, a pupil of the new mission school, who started the movement towards America. He is said to have landed in New York in 1834. He was followed by another student (1837), who obtained a medical degree from Princeton and then returned to practise in Constantinople. In 1841 one of the servants of Dr. D wight, a missionary, settled in Brooklyn. In the same year Rev. Haroutoon Vahabedian, who later became a Patriarch, entered the Union Theological School. Through the influence of other American missionaries two more students came to this country in 1843 and went to Yale. One of them, Christopher der Seropian, is said to have inaugurated the Class Book custom at Yale, and he is also credited with having discovered the black and green colors now used on all United States paper currency. In 1845 Serop Alishan, brother of Father Alishan, the distinguished Armenian poet, reached America. Between 1848-1849 an Armenian merchant, another student and two other Armenians came to the United States.

The number of Armenians arriving in America during the next twenty years (18501870) totals about fifty-five. A few of these were students, but the majority came here to learn trades. This

---

[16] The Armenian version of the Bible was first printed in Holland in 1666.

notable change of purpose was probably due to the late Dr. Cyrus Hamlin, founder of Robert College in Constantinople, who was a strong exponent of teaching the natives in Turkey modern methods of industry. The student class studied medicine and dentistry, and in this connection I might mention Doctors Simon Minasian, Calousdian and Bornig Mataosian, who served in the hospitals in Philadelphia during the Civil War.

There are also accounts of some Armenian volunteer soldiers and an orderly who fought in the ranks of the Northern Army. Most of the Armenians of this period, however, devoted themselves to learn trades. The well-known Hagop Mataosian, whose printing and publishing house in Constantinople is the largest and best in Turkey, was one of them. It was at this time, too, that for the first time three Armenian girls came to the United States. An old Armenian resident in New York states in a letter that in 1863 (fifty-five years ago), there were about ten Armenians in America who, with the exception of two or three, lived in New York City. In 1875 this number increased to about seventy, most of them being in New York and the rest scattered in the following cities: Jersey City, Worcester, Boston, Providence, Troy, Springfield, Lowell and Rochester, and one had gone as far as the Pacific Coast.

The next twenty-four years (1870-1894) brought a noticeable increase in the number of Armenians coming to this country. By this time the American Board of Commissioners for Foreign Missions had gradually expanded its activities throughout Turkey. It had founded colleges, high schools, primary schools and churches not only in Constantinople but also in other cities like Smyrna, Adana, Marash, Diarbekir, Harpout, Marsovan and Sivas. The increase of American missionary work brought with it a corresponding increase of Armenian immigration to the United States. A total of between thirty-five and forty Armenian students, at various times in this period (1870-1894), were enrolled at Yale, Princeton, Union, Andover, Amherst,

Wisconsin, New York University and Clark University. During this period, too, the United States became a place of sanctuary for Armenian political refugees. The Huntchaggist movement was started in 1883 and many of its leaders fled to America to escape persecution.

From the foregoing brief account covering a period of 60 years (1834-1894), certain interesting conclusions are to be drawn. In the first place, it is quite evident that the first Armenians who came here were not immigrants in the real sense of the word. They belonged to the wide-awake, ambitious and educated class. They came here to go to school, to learn trades, to engage in commerce, and a few to escape political persecution, but with the intention of returning to their country within a short time. The second important conclusion is that the idea of coming to the United States was due wholly to the American missionaries. The third point to note is that there were not more than three thousand Armenians actually residing in the United States in 1894. These came from a dozen or more different localities or cities in Turkey and founded small settlements in New York, Worcester, Boston, Providence, Hartford, Philadelphia, Hoboken, Troy, Chicago and Fresno, Cal., which cities in later years, as we shall see in the next chapter, became centers of the present great Armenian colonies[17].

---

[17] For the names, dates and accounts of the Armenians who came to the United States from 1834 to 1874, I am especially indebted to Archbishop Seropian.

Chapter III

IMMIGRATION AND DISTRIBUTION

IN this chapter we shall consider the number of Armenians in America to-day, the countries from which they came, who furnished the money for their passage, how many have been debarred, how many have voluntarily departed from the United States, and in what proportion those remaining here are distributed in the various states of the Union.

The principal sources of data on the specific topics enumerated in the preceding paragraph are the statistics of the Bureau of Immigration, the reports of the Immigration Commission and the eleventh census of the United States. While the information contained in these exhaustive volumes undoubtedly meets the essential requirements for which they were intended, yet they are deficient in respect to facts on particular immigrant races. In the absence of anything better, however, we are obliged to rely upon them constantly.

Up to 1898 the Bureau of Immigration classified immigrants according to the country of their birth or origin and not according to their race or language. For example a Turk, an Armenian, a Greek, a Jew or a Bulgarian coming from the Ottoman Empire was put down as an immigrant from Turkey. Consequently there are no accurate statistics touching the Armenians as a distinct class of immigrants prior to 1899. The figures employed here by me for the period between 1834 to and including 1898 are based upon a careful analysis of such general statistics as are available, together with an eye on surrounding historical circumstances and the opinions of the oldest members of the various Armenian colonies in this country. The task of compiling figures for the years following 1898 has been made a little easier because since that time the Department of Immigration, pursuant to an Act of Congress, established the practical system of classifying immigrants by their race.

IMMIGRATION FROM TURKEY TO THE UNITED STATES (1834-1894)[18]

Year	Turkey in Europe	Turkey in Asia	Year	Turkey in Europe	Turkey in Asa
1834	1		1864	14	
1835			1866	18	
1836	3		1867	26	
1837			1868	4	
1838			1869	18	2
1839	1		1870	6	
1840	1		1871	23	4
1841	6		1872	50	
1842	2		1873	53	3
1843	5		1874	62	6
1844	10		1875	27	1
1845	3		1876	38	8
1846	4		1877	32	3
1847	2		1878	29	7
1848	3		1879	29	31

---

[18] It will be noticed that from 1834-1894, a period of 60 years, the total number of immigrants from Turkey is 9472. What were the nationality of these is not known. They may have been Greeks, Bulgarians, Syrians, as well as Armenians. My opinion is that of this number about 4,000 only were Armenians, of whioh 1,000 returned to Turkey, leaving about 3,000 in the United States in 1894.

41

1849	9		1880	24	4
1850	15		1881	72	5
1851	2		1882	69	
1852	3		1883	86	
1853	15		1884	150	
1854	7		1885	138	
1855	9		1886	176	15
1856	5		1887	206	208
1857	11		1888	207	273
1858	17		1889	252	593
1859	10		1890	206	1126
1860	4		1891	265	2488
1861	5		1892	1331	
1862	11		1893	625	
1863	16		1894	298	
1864	11				

Total from Turkey in Asia, 4777
Total from Turkey in Europe, 4695
Grand Total   9472

NUMBER OF ARMENIANS ADMITTED INTO THE UNITED STATES (1895-1917)[19]

	Admitted				
Year	Male	Female	Total	Debarred	Departed
1895	a	a	2767c	b	b
1896	2915	1224	4139c	b	b
1897	3203	1532	4732c	b	b
1898	2615	1624	4275c	b	b
1899	471	203	674	30	b
1900	748	234	982	22	b
1901	1364	491	1855	21	b
1902	946	205	1151	18	b
1903	1424	335	1759	59	b
1904	1315	430	1745	48	b
1905	1339	539	1878	80	b
1906	1423	472	1895	64	b
1907	1874	770	2644	85	b
1908	2097	1202	3299	146	234
1909	2595	513	3108	94	561
1910	4686	822	5508	327	521
1911	2643	449	3092	319	901
1912	4476	746	5222	280	718
1913	7898	1460	9353	348	676
1914	6533	1252	7785	415	1250
1915	685	247	932	67	199

---

[19] Compiled from the annual reports of the United States Commission of Immigration, (a) Sex not given, (b) number not given, (c) race not given; but no doubt they were Armenians leaving Turkey on account of the massacres of 1894-96.

1916	775	189	964	49	659
1917	1017	204	1221	5	133
	53,073	15,140	70,980	2477	5852

Armenian immigration to the United States, in the strictest sense of the word, commenced immediately after the massacres of 1894. Before that time I think there were not over three thousand Armenians actually residing in this country. The United States Government statistics show that prior to 1895 there were very few persons coining here from Turkey in Asia where the majority of the Armenians lived. But suddenly in 1895, 2,767 were admitted from that part of the world, 4,189 in 1896, 4,732 in 1897 and 4,275 in 1898. Although these figures do not indicate the nationality of these 15,913, still there cannot be any doubt that they were nearly all Armenians leaving their homes on account of the massacres. Beginning with the year 1899 a system of keeping immigration records by races was installed. These records show that 55,057 more Armenians have come to the United States between 1899 and June 30, 1917, making 70,980 in all since 1894. To this figure should be added 3,000 for those who were here before 1894, making a total of 73,980. Of this number about 5,000 should be deducted for those who have died during this
period (1894-1917), and about 6,000 for those who have departed from the United States, leaving a balance of 62,980. And if we add to this number about 15,000 children born in this country of Armenian parents we would have a total of 77,980 Armenians in the United States to-day.

ARMENIANS ADMITTED INTO THE UNITED STATES FROM SPECIFIC COUNTRIES ' BETWEEN 1899 AND JUNE 80, 1917

Austria-Hungary	43	Switzerland	19
Belgium	12	Turkey in Europe	2,806
Bulgaria	158	Turkey in Asia	43,668
France	877	Great Britain	914
Germany	41	China	10
Greece	275	India	88
Italy	40	Africa (Egypt)	894
Netherlands	2	Australia	4
Norway	3	Canada	1,577
Portugal	4	Mexico	8
Roumania	95	South America	822
Russia	3,034	West Indies	18
Spain	5	Other Countries	189
Sweden	1		

Compiled from the annual reports of the Commission of Immigration,. 1899-1917.

One of the tables in this chapter denotes the countries from which the 55,057 admitted into the United States, between 1899 and 1917, came. These figures indicate that the influx of Armenian immigration has been principally from Turkey, with 43,668 to her credit. Russia is next with 8,034. There were 1,577 from Canada, 914 from Great Britain, 694 from Egypt, 822 from South America, 327 from France, 275 from Greece, 158 from Bulgaria, and less than a hundred each from Germany, Austria-Hungary, Spain, Sweden, Switzerland, India, Australia, Mexico, West Indies and other countries. I believe that the majority of those reported as having come from Canada, Great Britain, Egypt and France merely passed through these countries on their way to the United States.

Considerable importance is often attached to who furnishes the money for the transportation of immigrants to the United States and what is the financial status of an immigrant at the time of his landing in this country. According to the statistics 79.8 per cent of the Armenians pay their own expenses, 19.6 per cent receive aid from relatives and .5 per cent from other sources[20]. The form of the question asked by the Immigration examiners on this matter does not usually elicit the correct and desired answer. Technically speaking, most immigrants pay for their own passage, but as a matter of fact a large percentage of them borrow the necessary funds from friends and relatives in America. The table below indicates the average per capita amount of money shown by immigrants when they come to the United States[21].

Armenian	$81.67
Bulgarian and Servian	19.28
Croatian-Slovanian	16.14
Greek	24.10
Hebrew	29.09
Italian (South)	17.14
Polish	14.76
Roumanian	16.82
Ruthenian	14.89
Slovak	16.54
Syrian	45.42

---

[20] Report of the Immigration Commission. Statistical Review. Vol. Ill, page 361.
[21] Reports of the Immigration Commission, Statistical Review, Vol. Ill, page 350.

In the last ten years about 5,852 Armenians have departed from the United States for other countries against 40,484 admitted in the same period, or an average of about 14 to every hundred. Among other races the average number leaving this country for every hundred coming in is as follows: Bulgarians, 28; Greeks, 25; Syrians, 26; Turks, 69[22]. It would seem that among the principal races of immigrants from the Near East and the Balkans, the Armenians show less disposition to leave the United States.

A certain number of immigrants are debarred for a variety of causes, such as insanity, disease, prostitution and contract labor. It is to the credit of the Armenians to say that there are practically no prostitutes among them. The contract labor and padrone system are not known. Nearly all of those deported are returned because of Trachoma, an eye disease. During the last nineteen years only 2,477 Armenians have been refused admission.

I have had personal experience with immigration authorities on deportation cases. They give too hasty, too severe, and too technical interpretation of the Laws. Many immigrants have been sent back on the charge of prostitution or contract labor, whereas a broad, common sense understanding of the facts in each particular case and a knowledge of the customs and habits of each particular race, would have resulted in a different conclusion.

---

[22] Reports of the Immigration Commission, Statistical Review, Vol. Ill, page 383.

NUMBER OF ARMENIANS WHEN LANDING INDICATING INTENTION OF GOING TO THE STATES SPECIFIED[23] (1899-1917)

Alabama	58	Montana	5
Alaska	8	Nebraska	18
Arizona	8	Nevada	1
Arkansas	1	New Hampshire	522
California	2,564	New Jersey	2,115
Colorado	61	New Mexico	1
Connecticut	1,580	New York	17,391
District of Columbia	28	North Carolina	8
Florida	18	Ohio	401
Georgia	8	Oklahoma	7
Hawaii	1	Oregon	15
Idaho	8	Pennsylvania	2,002
Illinois	8,813	Porto Rico	4
Indiana	167	Rhode Island	4,923
Iowa	82	South Carolina	1
Kansas	11	South Dakota	13
Kentucky	11	Tennessee	8
Louisiana	10	Texas	268
Maine	547	Utah	65
Maryland	48	Vermont	41
Massachusetts	14,192	Virginia	138
Michigan	1,371	Washington	71
Minnesota	67	West Virginia	28
Mississippi	6	Wisconsin	1,184
Missouri	649	Wyoming	2

[23] Compiled from the annual reports of the Commission of Immigration, 1890-1917.

Before an immigrant is permitted to leave the port of landing, he is required to state where he intends to go directly. Out of a total of 55,057 Armenians who have come here since 1899, 17,391 indicated their intention of going to New York State, 14,192 to Massachusetts, 4,928 to Rhode Island, 3,818 to Illinois, 2,564 to California, 2,115 to New Jersey, 2,002 to Pennsylvania, 1,580 to Connecticut, 1,371 to Michigan, and 1,184 to Wisconsin, and less than 1,000 each to other states. While those figures give some idea of the principal states where Armenians congregate, they must not be taken as showing the actual number of Armenians in each such state. There is always a shifting of population, and among the Armenians there has been a steady and growing migration to California, where there are more of them than in any other state. The largest single Armenian colony is in New York City, and the next largest is in Fresno, Cal., and then follow Worcester, Boston, Philadelphia, Chicago, West Hoboken, Jersey City, Detroit, Los Angeles, Troy and Cleveland[24].

----

[24] The following is a more complete list of Armenian colonies in the United States having more than 100 persons: California – Fresno, Reedley, Yettem, Salema, Los Angeles, Sanger,

Fowler. Connecticut – Hartford, Thompsonville, New Haven, New Britain, Bridgeport. Illinois – Chicago, Waukegan, East St. Louis. Indiana – Indianapolis. Kentucky – Louisville. Maine – Portland.

Massachusetts – Boston, Worcester, Lynn, Lowell, Lawrence, Haverhill, Hopedale, Middleboro, Maiden, Newton Upper Falls, Newburyport, Whitinsville, Watertown, Chelsea, Brockton, Bridgewater, Salem,

Somerville, Springfield, Peabody, Cambridge, Fitchburg, Franklin. Minnesota. – St. Paul. Missouri – St. Louis.

Michigan – Highland Park, Detroit, Grand Rapids. Maryland – Baltimore. New Hampshire – Manchester, Nashua. New York – Schenectady, Yonkers, Niagara Falls, New York, Binghamton,

Brooklyn, Syracuse, Rochester, Messina Springs.

ley – Un" Newark.

New Jersey – Union Hill, West Hoboken, Jersey City, Summit, Paterson, Ohio – Akron, Toledo, Cleveland, Cincinnati.

Oregon – Portland.

Chapter IV

CAUSES OF IMMIGRATION

IT was the presence of and contact with the American missionaries in Turkey that started the movement of Armenian emigration to the United States. Before Doctors Goodell, Dwight and Schauffler of the Board of Commissioners for Foreign Missions settled in Constantinople in 1831, we have no record of any Armenians coming to the United States, except those who were in Virginia back in the seventeenth century. In 1834 one of the students of the Bible study class formed by these missionaries at Bebek (a suburb of Constantinople) reached New York. From that time up to 1874 the seventy or more who followed him to this country were in some way connected with the newly established Protestant communities and schools of the American missionaries. In the beginning they came chiefly from Constantinople, but as soon as the Americans extended their operations to other cities such as Nicomedea (near Brousa), Smyrna, Aintab, Adana, Marash, it soon resulted in stirring Armenians from these places also towards the New World. Aside from the fact that the going of the Americans to the various cities in Turkey preceded the coming of the Armenians from those cities to the United States, there are also the reports, publications

---

Pennsylvania – Philadelphia.
Rhode Island – Providence, Woonsocket, Pawtucket.
Vermont – Winooski.
Virginia – Richmond, Hopeville, City Point.
District of Columbia – Washington.
Washington – Seattle.
Wisconsin – Madison, Milwaukee, Kenosha, and Racine.

and correspondence of the missionaries in which one frequently meets with the names of the early Armenians who came to this country.

Up to about 1880 there were so few Armenians in the United States that it has been possible to prepare a more or less complete list of their names. But when the Sultan began to persecute the Huntchaggist, a so-called revolutionary society, there was a decided increase, and while this increase was due to the prevailing political unrest that culminated in the massacres of 1894, 1895 and 1896, still the reason why those who fled chose the United States as a place of refuge instead of France, England or Switzerland is unquestionably found in the influence of the American missionaries.

Immigration of the Armenians to the

United States, in the real sense of that phrase, commenced immediately after the massacres. During the preceding sixty years (1834-1894) , I believe a total of about four thousand Armenians had come to this country. But in 1895 over four thousand were admitted in one year, and this number has since steadily gone upward, until it reached nearly eight thousand for the fiscal year ending January 30, 1914. Mr. William Eleroy Curtis, the distinguished correspondent of the Chicago Herald, writing from Turkey under date of September 11, 1910, gives the following graphic account:

"The congregation of the American Churches and especially the pupils of the missionary schools, are usually reduced from 25 to 30 per cent every year by immigration to the United States. Having learned from their teachers of the advantages and the opportunities that exist across the water; having acquired the English language and being able to get good advices as to location and often letters of introduction, they have decided advantages over ordinary emigrants and for that reason they make the best sort at citizens when they reach their new home.

"A dozen missionaries have told me that the brightest and most promising young men and women in their district, and especially the best teachers in their schools have emigrated. For example, the church at Harpout had 3,107 members one year and 2,413 the next. The balance had gone to America. One-fourth of the congregation of the mission church at Bitlis emigrated almost in a body last year. It would be a great deal better for Turkey if these people would stay at home and use the knowledge and principles they have gained in the regeneration of their country; but it cannot be denied that they are among the most valuable immigrants of all the aliens that go to the United States."

Another incident contributed materially towards increasing the volume of Armenian immigration after the massacres. The coldblooded murder of over 100,000 Christians aroused the sympathy of the American public to such a degree that their kindness towards Armenians already here and the welcome the refugees received were unprecedented. Churches, clubs, charitable societies vied with one another to clothe and feed them and to find suitable homes and profitable employment for them. The immigrants wrote home describing the wonders of the New World and the generosity of the American people. The effect of these letters was dynamic. Friends, relatives and neighbors, hearing of the luck of those who had come here and having before them the unsettled condition of their own country, decided at once to emigrate to the land of "gold and honey."

There is still another cause. In 1908 Sultan Abdul Hamid was dethroned and a Constitutional Monarchy established in Turkey. Before this change took place Christians were excluded from the army and a tax was imposed on them in lieu of military service. Under this new law Christians were inducted into the army. For obvious reasons the Armenians did not look upon this with favor or pride and therefore many young men of military age left the country and came to America.

The causes of Armenian immigration from Turkey to the United States may be summarized as follows: It was started through the influence of the American missionaries. Subsequently the inauguration of persecution by the Sultan of Armenian leaders and the Armenians in general upon the pretense of suppressing a "revolution" added largely to the annual number of those who were coming here. The massacres of 1894-1895-1896 finally forced thousands to seek the United States for safety. The welcome and comparatively better and brighter opportunities found in this country by the refugees encouraged others to emigrate also. In particular the young men came here to escape military service, or to go to school or to engage in some business. The young women came principally to marry. There were those, of course, who immigrated because of the unsettled and unsafe political conditions and general poverty in their native land. A few have come to join friends and relatives, and still others because it had become the "style" in certain localities to go to America.

Chapter V

THE ARMENIANS IN INDUSTRIES

THE statistics I have tabulated from the reports of the Commissioner of Immigration disclose certain valuable data concerning the industrial character of the Armenians. They show that among these people the percentage of skilled laborers and professional men is greater than among any other race of immigrants coming from Southeastern Europe and the Ottoman possessions in Asia. Since 1899, 55,057 Armenians have been admitted into the United States. Of these, 14,020 were skilled workmen representing forty-nine kinds of trades; 1,281 were farmers; 782 were professional men, teachers, lawyers, doctors, clergymen, engineers, artists and writers, and 1,161 were merchants, manufacturers, bankers and agents. The next table presents more forcibly the relative superiority of the Armenians in this respect when compared with other so-called newer immigrant peoples.

	Professional	Skilled Laborers	Farm Laborers	Laborers	In other Occupations
Armenians	2.3	39.5	23.5	17.8	17.1
Bulgarians	.1	3.3	47.7	44.3	4.6
Greeks	.3	7.7	19.4	66.8	5.8
Irish	1.3	12.6	4.6	30.6	50.9
Polish	.2	6.3	30.5	44.8	18.1
Roumanians	.2	2.7	59.4	34.4	3.8
Syrians	1.2	22.7	29.7	21.1	25.3

Reports of the Immigration Commission Statistical Review, Vol. Ill, page 96.

OCCUPATIONS OF 55,057 ARMENIAN IMMIGRANTS WHEN ADMITTED INTO THE UNITED STATES (1899-1917)

PROFESSIONAL

Actors	18	Musicians	17
Architects	17	Officials (Government)	7
Clergy	107	Physicians	35
Editors	20	Sculptors & Artists	32
Electricians	17	Teachers	334
Engineers	42	Others	84
Lawyers	12	Total	782
Literary persons	40		

SKILLED

Bakers	445	Cigarette makers	3
Barbers	718	Cigar makers	3
Blacksmiths	720	Cigar packers	1
Bookbinders	22	Clerks & Accountants 423	
Brewers	1	Dressmakers	120
Butchers	205	Engineers	71
Cabinetmakers	20	Engravers	11

Carpenters	1419	Furriers	11
Gardeners	80	Saddlers & Harness makers	35
Halters	5		
Iron & Steel Workers	474	Seamstresses	211
Jewelers	195	Shoemakers	8594
Locksmiths	72	Stokers	52
Machinists	110	Stonecutters	48
Mariners	47	Tailors	2267
Masons	254	Tanners	106
Metal Workers	176	Textile makers	85
Millers	25	Tinners	149
Milliners	10	Tobacco	60
Miners	28	Upholsterers	20
Painters & Glaziers	141	Watchmakers	96
Photographers	58	Weavers	950
Plasterers	6	Wheelwrights	8
Plumbers	6	Woodworkers	15
Printers	62	Other skilled	887
		Total	14,026

MISCELLANEOUS

Agents	28	Manufacturers	8
Bankers	9	Merchants	1,117
Drymen	18	Servants	3,386
Farm laborers	10,697	Others	416
Farmers	1,281	Total	27,806
Hotel keepers	17		
Laborers	10,829		
No Occupation			
Women & Children			12,443
Grand Total[25]			55,057

---

[25] Compiled from the annual reports of the Commissioner of Immigration.

Even though the Armenians come here well equipped for industrial purposes, still the task of finding suitable employment under the conditions existing in the United States is beset with many difficulties and hardships. The skill and experience many possess in some particular trade or handicraft is not usually an asset in earning a livelihood here. In the old country all commodities, if not imported from England, France, Germany and America, are made by hand, while here in America practically every article in daily use is produced by machinery with which the Armenians are absolutely unfamiliar. They are further handicapped because they are regarded as "foreigners," many are excluded from Trade Unions, and their ignorance of the English language as well as of the customs of the country so unlike those to which they had been accustomed for centuries, aggravates the difficulties they are bound to encounter. On the other hand those who have a small capital dare not start a business of their own, as they might have done in their native land, on account of the serious competition and disadvantages they must face. The educated and the professional class also discover that their learning is not only a drop in a bucket but far inferior to the standard required here. Thus with rare exceptions all Armenian immigrants are obliged to commence life in the New World by undertaking some sort of manual labor. Whatever success they attain in future years is due purely to their native ambition and intelligence.

We have seen in a preceding chapter that while Armenians have settled in nearly every state in the Union, still ninety per cent of them are located in New York, Massachusetts, Rhode Island, Connecticut, Pennsylvania, Illinois, Michigan, Wisconsin and California. It is therefore to them that we must turn our attention.

In the New England States, in Boston, Lynn, Lowell, Haverhill, Brockton, Salem, Peabody, Nashua, Springfield, Worcester, Whitinsville, Hartford, Providence, Woonsocket, etc., they work in the shoe factories, in the iron foundries, in the machine shops, and in the woolen mills. Almost the entire colony in Troy is engaged in the shirt and collar industry. In Paterson and West Hoboken, N. J., they are employed in the silk mills. It is difficult to say what is their principal occupation in New York City. Some are in the oriental rug repairing trade, others work in mercantile houses, many are waiters in the best hotels and restaurants; the Pennsylvania Railroad Company uses a large number as porters, and a still larger number of them are scattered in hundreds of other occupations so abundant in such a city as New York. Throughout Pennsylvania Armenians have been found not only in the mills and factories in Philadelphia, but also in the bituminous coal mines. In the cities of the middle west such as Cleveland, Akron, Grand Rapids, St. Louis, East St. Louis, Chicago, they work in the great iron and steel shops, in the automobile and furniture manufacturing establishments and in the slaughter houses.

The Armenian workmen in these industries have rightfully earned the reputation of being among the most industrious in our heterogeneous laboring population. Years of oppression and struggle for existence against untold economic barriers have made them accustomed to hard work. Temperance is the prevailing habit among them because beer, whiskey and other forms of expensive intoxicating liquors are unknown in Armenia. Moreover, every Armenian immigrant has some dependent to support, such as a father, mother, sister or wife and children. All these things add to their efficiency as laborers and explain the reason why they stand foremost in their capacity to earn comparatively high wages. The Immigration Commission reports[26] that in the manufacturing industries the average weekly earnings of an Armenian is $9.73; of a Greek, $8.41; of a Syrian,

---

[26] Reports of the Immigration Commission. Abstract of Reports Vol. I, pages 367, 375, 407 and 412. These figures relate to conditions prior to the war.

$8.12. The table below shows by races the annual average income of workmen.

Armenians	$454	Roumanians	$402
Bulgarians	255	Russians	400
Greeks	800	Servians	212
Lithuanians	454	Slovak	442
Magyar	395	Syrians	370
Polish	428	Turks	281

The average annual income of an Armenian family composed of wage-earners was found to be $730; that of a Greek family, $632; a Hebrew family, $685; North Italian, $657; South Italian, $569; Servian, $462; Lithuanian, $636; Polish, $595; Russian, $494; Ruthenian, $569; Slovak, $582, and Syrian, $594.

Next in importance to the Armenians working in the manufacturing and mining industries in the eastern states, there are the Armenian farmers in California. The Immigration Commission made a special study of the colony in Fresno which deserves to be quoted.

"The Settlement and Progbess of the Armenian Farmers"[27]

"More interest attaches to the immigration, activities and progress of the Armenian farmers than those of any other race, save the Japanese, found in Fresno County. The extent of their holdings and the place they occupy in the agricultural industries have already been noted and do not call for further comment in this place.

••

---

[27] Reports of the Immigration Commission. Immigrants in Industries* Part 25, Vol. II, page 633.

"The Armenians about Fresno differ from other immigrants found there in that they have not been drawn from agricultural classes to any great extent, nor have they been drawn from the class of common laborers. These classes have been oppressed in their native land but have generally been able to emigrate. The emigrants have been for the greater part merchants, commission men, craftsmen, small shopkeepers, shoemakers, silk weavers, dyers, coppersmiths, and men of that type have been most numerous who in their native land combined handicraft manufacture and small shop-keeping, a system still prevalent in Armenia.

"These Armenians brought with them any wealth they had accumulated. In some cases this was sufficient to constitute a working capital and enable them to start in business. In the majority of cases, however, they came with little or nothing. Such immigrants usually found employment in shoe factories in Massachusetts, in silk mills in New Jersey, or in iron and steel mills. Those who migrated directly to Fresno found employment in the packing houses and as farm laborers for the most part. But such persons were exceptional. The vast majority migrated to Fresno after spending years in Armenian colonies in the eastern industrial centers. However, they sooner or later desired to leave the factory life which was undermining their physique. Those who moved West were attracted to the new Armenian colony which enjoyed favorable climate and good opportunities. Many of them, like the Danes, purchased land and at once became independent farmers upon settling in the new community. The Armenians have, in fact, shown a desire for land not less strong than that of the Japanese. Being ambitious, disliking the wage relation, and being compelled to stand apart as a race, they have had as their goal the establishment of a business or independent farming. Furthermore, like the Japanese, they are quite willing to take great risk where profit may be made.

"In 1900 the number of tenant farmers in Fresno County was very large. White men had the tenure of 3,214 farms. Of these 436 were leased for a share of the crop and 294 for a cash rental. A considerable number of these tenants were no doubt Armenians who had begun to farm on their own account and who then leased a larger percentage of the land they farmed than they do now. In some cases this was a stepping-stone to the purchasing of farms. But at present the Armenians rank next to the Japanese as leasing farmers. Much of the land leased, however, is in addition to farms owned and cultivated by them.

"The Armenians have invested much of their savings in various enterprises in the City of Fresno. More of them have been invested in farm lands, however. They have been so desirous to purchase, in fact, that they have at times bid up prices beyond what the land was really worth as a means of making a living and accumulating property. This fact and the further fact that they have usually bought soils good for viticulture, and frequently if not generally, with bearing vines, explain the fact that the Armenians have paid a higher price per acre for the farms purchased by them than any other race investigated. For 16 farms they paid from $39.38 to $300 per acre, the average price being $179.94.

"The Armenians, like other races about Fresno, have usually paid cash in part and have given a mortgage on the land for the larger part of the purchase price. Taking 16 of the farms investigated as typical . . . the total of the purchase price of $143,950. . . . Of this $52,150 was paid in cash, $91,800 covered by mortgage. In one instance the full amount was paid in cash. At the other extreme $200 was paid on a purchase price of $4,500. Thus most of the Armenian farmers have begun independent farming deeply in debt.

"All members of the Armenian family work on the ranch. They economize and save carefully. Some add to the profits of the farms the earnings obtained in packing houses or near-by ranches. Yet such labor is not general. Little of the surplus made is sent abroad; little is used to improve their houses. On the contrary, the savings are used to pay off mortgage indebtedness, or to buy more land, or is sunk in improvements in the land. They are most successful in developing farms, making money, and paying off mortgage indebtedness.

"By working hard, by living frugally, and by good management, the Armenians have usually succeeded better than any other race in accumulating property. Not even the Japanese about Fresno have succeeded as well as they. The 16 farmers who reported complete data (and they are believed to be typical of the land-owing Armenians of the country) had properties with a gross value of about $300,000. The value of the real estate was estimated at $246,150, against which there was mortgage indebtedness aggregating $79,825, or roughly one-third of the somewhat exaggerated estimate values[28]. They have few other

[28] The following account is given in another part of the Reports of the Immigration Commission:

"The Armenian Farmers. The chief Armenian colony in the West is in Fresno County, Cal. The members of this race have been settling here for twenty-five years, and including the native-born element, now number more than 4,000. About one half live in Fresno, the others in the country, where the majority are tenant or land-owning farmers. Ambitious and disliking the wage relation, they usually quickly establish themselves in business or as farmers. At present it is estimated that they have the tenure of possibly 25,000 acres of land, at least three-fifths of which they own. They have usually purchased or leased vineyards and orchards. It is estimated that they control between 16,000 and 20,000 acres, or roughly one-sixth of the acreage devoted to the production of raisin grapes. They grow some fruit, and from 5 to 10 per cent of the watermelons shipped from the county. They have shown an even greater ambition to secure land than have the Japanese, and have frequently 'bid up' the price of land in order to secure possessions of desirable farms. They are very industrious, and by business shrewdness, – economy, have made rapid progress in the accumulation of wealth." Reports of Immigration Commission, Part 25, Vol. 2, Immigrants in Industries, page 296-7.

debts, however, so that the net value of their property wa3 $185,337.33 or an average of $11,587 per farmer. Of the 17, four had property valued at less than $5,000 (net) , 5 at between $5,000 and $10,000, 5 between $10,000 and $25,000; 2 more than $25,000, while one did not report the exact amount. Settling in the immediate localities and purchasing land at various dates, beginning with 1900, in 1908 the selected farmers had between three and four times as much property as they had at the time of their settlement."

Since this report was made the Armenians have more than tripled their holdings in California.

Besides the workingmen in the mills and factories, and those engaged in agricultural pursuits, there is a third important class of Armenians, viz., the small tradesmen. In all Armenian centers there are the grocers, tailors and shoemakers. It is reported that in the City of New York there are over 500 repairing and tailor shops, about an equal number of shoe-repairing stores (shoe-shining "parlors" are conducted almost exclusively by the Greeks) , and over 500 grocers. The same situation is true in other cities where Armenians have settled in large numbers. There are, of course, scores of clothiers, jewelers, barbers, restaurant keepers, etc.

I have pointed out in another part of this book that ninety per cent of the Armenians in the United States to-day have come here within the last twenty-five years. They have not, therefore, had sufficient time to undertake great business enterprises. But what individuals have accomplished in the line of commerce and manufacture is really worthy of mention. Armenians have commenced to enter the clothing manufacturing business. There are Armenians engaged in making candies, in the printing business, in manufacturing jewelry, machinery, tools, shoes and in the cleaning and dyeing business and in laundry work. Some of the best photo-engraving establishments in New York City are conducted by Armenians. Zoolak, Matzoon, Fermilac and other forms of fermented milk called under different names was first introduced in the United States by Armenians. Armenians are also interested in the manufacture of silk goods, machine-made embroideries and carpets. There are a considerable number engaged in the export and import business.

The oriental rug business has attracted the attention of many Armenians. A half dozen Armenian merchants in New York City import annually into the United States nearly seventy per cent of these carpets into this country. Although some Greek and American capital has been invested in recent years in this business, still the Armenians are the leaders. They have factories in New Jersey where the rugs are washed so as to subdue their original brilliant color and thus make them marketable in America. They are the best buyers in the Eastern markets because they know and understand how to deal with the natives there. Beside the large Armenian importing houses, there are the small retail traders in nearly every city of importance throughout the country. These concerns usually purchase from the importers a stock of rugs either for cash or on consignment and sell them to the public. The reputation of some of these smaller oriental carpet or rug dealers has suffered, I think, unjustly. An oriental rug is a work of art; it is like a painting. Its value depends not so much upon what it originally cost the buyer, but more upon its value to the purchaser. One buys a rug for a certain price, say $250, and subsequently shows it to some one who says it is worth $200 – that is the value of the article to him; but the purchaser thinks he has been deceived.

There are also Armenians in the professions. I believe there are in this country over one hundred Armenian Protestant clergymen and at least fifty of these preach in English to American congregations. The number of Armenian doctors and dentists in the United States exceeds two hundred and a large number of them have a good American practice, in fact the very best of these doctors and dentists do not have many clients among the

Armenians. Armenian lawyers now in active practice number about fifteen. These are located in New York, Boston, Providence, Philadelphia, Jersey City, Los .Angeles and Fresno. Two or three of them have succeeded in building up a lucrative practice among American or non-Armenian clients. There are a great many engineers, chemists and architects. There are about eight Armenian professors and instructors in American colleges and universities. The Professor of Oral Military Surgery at the Harvard Dental School, one of the Associate Professors of Organic Chemistry at Lehigh, an Assistant Professor of Physics at the University of Pennsylvania, the assistant Librarian and Lecturer on oriental languages at the Hartford Theological School, an instructor of chemistry at Yale, an instructor in the medical school of the University of Michigan, are Armenians. Two of the most noted photographers in the United States are Armenians. There are well-known Armenian painters and sculptors in New York, Chicago and San Francisco. There are Armenians on the stage and distinguished operatic singers, one of whom often appears at the Metropolitan Opera House in New York.

Mr. Arshag Mahdesian, the editor of New Armenia, has furnished me with the following interesting memorandum relative to Armenians who have won distinction in America.

"The Armenians have not been less prominent in the United States: witness the late Governor Thomas Corwin[29], of Ohio, also at one time Secretary of the United States Treasury; the late Dr. Mihran K. Kassabian, the distinguished scientist of Philadelphia, and one of the foremost Roentgen rays investigators in the world; Dr. Menas Gregory, the eminent psychiatrist of Bellevue Hospital, New York; Mooshegh Vaygouny, a graduate of the University of California, who developed a synthetic method of converting grape sugar into tartaric acid; Mugurdich Garo, the

[29] With reference to Governor Thomas Corwin see "Diversions of a Diplomat in Turkey," by Samuel Cox, page 182.

famous photographer of Boston, unquestionably one of the greatest in America, who originated the Garograph; M. Mangassarian, of Chicago, the eloquent exponent of liberal thought in America; Haig Patigian, the distinguished San Francisco sculptor, who was awarded the prize for executing a monument to commemorate the rebuilding of San Francisco; and Dr. Seropyan, the inventor of the green color of the American paper dollar. Even the first American soldier to land at Manila, in the SpanishAmerican war, was an Armenian, according to Nessib Behar, Managing Director of the National Liberal Immigration League."

Chapter VI

RELIGION AND EDUCATION

THE Armenians in the United States, have brought with them their religious institutions. These institutions fall into two principal groups, namely, the Armenian Apostolic Church, often spoken of as the Church of Arftienia or the Gregorian Church, and the Armenian Evangelical (Protestant) Church. The latter in turn is divided into Congregational and Presbyterian denominations, with the Congregationalists in the majority. It is estimated that about eighty per cent of the Armenians in this country belong to the Church of Armenia, about fifteen per cent are adherents of the Protestant churches and the rest compose the Catholic and other sects. These figures are not authentic as no statistics are available to verify them, but they are confirmed by the opinion of wellinformed Armenian clergymen.

It has been noted that the Armenian immigrants have congregated in certain industrial centers along the Atlantic coast, around the Great Lakes and on the Pacific. In all these centers the Armenian Gregorian and the Protestant communities each have their separate churches. For example, in Boston, Worcester[30], Lawrence, Lowell, Providence, Troy, New York, Hoboken, Philadelphia, Chicago, Los Angeles, Fresno, Fowler, Parlier and Yettem (Cal.), there is a Gregorian as well as a Protestant Church and with two or three exceptions the church buildings in all these cities are owned by their respective congregations. A large number of smaller and less prosperous communities have

---

[30] The first Armenian Apostolic Church and the first Armenian Protestant Church were built in Worcester, Mass.

missions and still smaller outlying districts are visited from time to time by Armenian pastors and rectors[31].

Some of the peculiarly local features of these immigrant churches will naturally interest a great many readers and I mention them here casually. Services of course are conducted in the Armenian language. For a few Armenians who come from Adana and Caesarea, and speak Turkish only, a special mission (Protestant) has been organized in Boston, and in other cities the Armenian Protestant churches hold services once a month or less often, in the Turkish language. Each church, whether Gregorian or Evangelical, elects by popular vote its trustees or deacons, as well as its rector or pastor as the case may be. Each Gregorian community pays the expenses of its church, but the Protestant churches receive substantial financial assistance from the State

---

[31] Rev. Mihron T. Kalaidjinn, Secretary of the Armenian Missionary Association of America, has given me the following memorandum:

"The Protestant Armenian churches, u great majority of # which are Congregational, are governed according to the polity and principles of the Congregational church, and at the same time are enjoying the benevolent care of the home missionary secretaries and societies. However, among these churches there are two organized bodies for the purpose of fellowship and mutual help and inspiration. One is the Armenian Evangelical Alliance of America, which takes in all of the Eastern and Middle Western States. At present it is composed of ten regularly organized churches and fourteen missions. Of these, one church and three missions are Presbyterian, one church is independent and the rest are Congregational. The other organization is the Armenian Evangelical Alliance of California, comprising six regularly organized churches and several missions. Two of these churches are Presbyterian and the rest Congregational. Five of these churches have their own houses of worship, and in this respect the Armenian churches of California are very fortunate. We see from the foregoing that the organized evangelical forces among the Armenians in this country consist altogether of fifteen churches and about twenty missions. The number of Gregorian churches in this country is fifteen, and occasional church services are held by visiting priests."

Home Missionary Societies and that is one reason why the Protestants, although constituting only fifteen per cent of the Armenian population in the United States, still have as many well organized churches as the Gregorians with their far larger membership. Some of the Armenian Apostolic Churches conduct a parochial school where children are taught their mother tongue, but these are rather poorly attended. Moreover, the Gregorian churches are under the authority and guidance of a Prelate[32], who is elected by the members through a representative assembly. The Prelate is the recipient of considerable prestige and power. He is the supreme head of the Armenian Apostolic Church in America.

The Armenian people have always been warm supporters of religion in general and their venerable church in particular. But here in the United States they manifest an apparent lack of interest. In this respect it is only fair to say that the Protestant churches are better attended. That is probably due to the fact that the pastors of the Protestant churches are better educated. Every one of them is a graduate of an American college and speaks English fluently. They have superior facilities for organization. Their sermons are well prepared and they have succeeded in making their churches centers of considerable religious and civic activities. On the other hand there are only two or three of the higher clergy of the Gregorian Church in this country, and the Derders (parish rectors), with few exceptions, are not as well educated as the pastors of Protestant churches. These Derders come here at an advanced age and never seem to grasp the changes that have taken place in the temper, outlook and

---

[32] The following have been the Prelates of the Armenian Apostolic Church in the United States, Hovsep V. Sara j any an 1899, Makhakia (Vartabed) Deroonian 1894, Mashtotz (Vartabed) Papazian 1897, Sarajyan (Yebisgobos) 1898, Moushed (Yebisgobos) Seropian 1911, Arsen (Vartabed) Vahooni, and the present incumbent is Shahcn (Vartabed) Kasparian. The official residence of the Prelate is at Worcester, Mass.

demands of the Armenian immigrants, and so adapt themselves and the churches to meet these changes. The people love their church, but cannot endure the long services, poor sermons and "church troubles" resulting from bad management and organization. They will pay their annual dues and if need be more; they will rally around their church when something threatens it, but will not attend services except on special occasion such as Christmas and Easter. The younger members of both Gregorian and Protestant families take little interest in their native ecclesiastical institutions. I believe more Armenians, both young and old, go to American churches than to their own.

Education

There are fewer illiterates among the Armenians than among any of the other so-called newer immigrant races. This remarkable fact – I call it remarkable because the Armenians have had no government of their own for five hundred years and any attempt they have made for advancement has been suppressed by the Sultans – is disclosed by the statistics of the United States Government. Of all the Armenians, men, women and children admitted into this country between 1899-1910, only 28.9 per cent could not read or write. The percentage of illiterates of other races of immigrants for the same period is as follows[33]: Bulgarian, 41.7; Greeks, 26.4; Hebrews, 26.0; Roumanians, 35.0; Southern Italians, 53.9; Polish, 35.4; Portuguese, 68.2; Russians, 38.4, and Syrians, 53.3. A few years ago the Immigration Commission made an exhaustive study of 500,329 workmen employed in a large number of manufacturing and mining industries all over the

---

[33] Report of the Immigration Commission. Abstract of Reports, Vol. I, page 99.

United States in which there were representatives of over two dozen races. This investigation shows that among the Armenian laborers 92.1 per cent could read and 90.5 could read and write; among the Bulgarians 78.1 per cent could read and 76.8 could read and write; among the Greeks 80.5 per cent could read and 79.5 per cent could read and write; among the Syrians 63.6 per cent could read and 62.0 per cent could read and write[34]. Certain classes of immigrants are well represented in California and the data collected there by the Immigration Commission on the subject of literacy is, therefore, quite complete. The Commission reports that "The Armenians, Germans and North Italians each show more than 95 per cent literates, or somewhat more than the average among the foreign born (91.4 per cent)[35]." Among the farm laborers the report states that "of the other numerically important races, the percentages of those who can read and write their native languages are as follows: North Italians, 95 per cent; Armenians, 94.7 per cent; Greeks, 91.9 per cent; Germans, 87 per cent; Chinese, 84.6 per cent; South Italians, 66.3 per cent; Mexicans, 50.5 per cent; East Indians, 44.9 per cent; and Portuguese, 41.4 per cent[36]." Among the females, "those having the largest percentages of literates were the Armenians with 84.9 per cent; the Germans, 75.3 per cent and the Japanese, 73.1 per cent[37].'

---

[34] Reports of the Immigration Commission, Abstracts of Reports, Vol. I, pages 438-442.

[35] Reports of the Immigration Commission Immigrants in Industries. Part 25, Vol. 2, page 69.

[36] Reports of the Immigration Commission. Immigrants in Industries. Part 25, Vol. II, page 65.

[37] Ibid., page 70.

OLD AND NEW IMMIGRANTS COMPARED WITH RESPECT TO ABILITY TO READ[38]

OLD IMMIGRANTS Percentage able to read		NEW IMMIGRANTS Percentage able to read	
Canadian (French)	88.1	Armenian	92.1
Canadian (others)	98.9	Bulgarian	78.1
Dutch	97.6	Greek	80.5
English	98.8	Lithuanian	77.8
German	98.0	Polish	79.9
Irish	95.8	Portuguese	47.5
Scotch	99.5	Roumanians	82.6
Swedish	99.8	Russian	74.5
Welsh	98.1	Servian Syrian	71.3 63.6

With reference to ability to speak, English among the farm laborers in California, and employees in the boot and shoe factories in the eastern cities, the Armenians were found to be ahead of other races. For instance, in California 64.9 per cent of those examined could speak English, while the percentage among other races was as follows: Greeks, 59.5 per cent; Germans, 43.5 per cent; South Italians, 40 per cent; North Italians, 22.6 per cent; and Mexicans, 21.7 per cent. The Armenian workmen in the boot and shoe industries showed even a greater percentage of those able to speak English with 82.9 per cent; Greeks, 65.5 per cent and Polish, 50.6 per cent[39].

---

[38] Ibid. Abstracts of Reports. Vol.1, page 443.
[39] Reports of the Immigration Commission. Part 25, Vol. 2, page 58; Also Part 8-10, page 439.

I believe it was J. Gordon Browne who once said that "The Armenian passion for education is astonishing. There is probably no people in the world who will make such sacrifice for this object." Here in America there is concrete illustration of the foregoing opinion. I have yet to meet Armenian parents, who, no matter how poor and ignorant they may be, do not regard the education of their children of the utmost importance. In 1909 there were 1,031 Armenians in the public schools of 37 American cities[40]. Unfortunately Hoboken,

N. J., and Fresno, Cal., where the Armenian colonies are very large, are not included in these cities. The table below shows the number of immigrants in the United States by race in 1910, the total number of children of each race in the public schools of 37 cities and the number of students in colleges and universities. I call the reader's special attention to the remarkable showing of the Armenians[41].

	Approximate number in the U.S. 1910	*Number of pupils in public schools of 37 cities 1908-9*	*Number of students colleges and in universities 1908-9*
Armenians	26,498	1,081	29
Bulgarians	97,391	504	10
Croatians	335,543	497	1
Greeks	216,962	1,002	13

[40] Number of Armenian pupils in the public schools of 37 cities (19081909): Boston 133, Chelsea 28, Chicago 15, Cincinnati 2, Cleveland 3, Detroit 4, Fall River 2, Haverhill 20, Los Angeles 37, Lowell 29, Lynn 63, Manchester 2, Milwaukee 2, Newark 9, New Bedford 3, New Britain 38, New York 190, Philadelphia 74, Pittsburg 2, Providence 153, St. Louis 9, San Francisco 3, Scranton 1, Worcester 197, Yonkers 12. – From the Reports of the Immigration Commission on Immigrants in the schools.

[41] Reports of the Immigration Commission, Abstracts of Reports. Vol. 2, pages 10-16.

Roumanians	82,704	1,265	9
Ruthenians	147,375	511	7
Syrians	56, 909	1, 281	17

The report of the Armenian Students' Association for the year 1916 shows over 250 students enrolled in the leading colleges and universities in the United States. While the Greek, Bulgarian, Servian, Roumanian and Syrian populations in America outnumber the Armenians by many thousands, still none of them have anywhere near as many students in the higher institutions of learning as the Armenians. Yale, Harvard, University of California, Chicago, Wisconsin, Michigan, Massachusetts Institute of Technology, Valparaiso, Columbia, Brown and Amherst are the principal colleges and universities that attract these young men and a few young women. Medicine seems to be their favorite profession. Architecture, chemistry, law, pedagogics, electrical engineering, agriculture, theology, mining, political economy, philosophy, dentistry, pharmacy and forestry follow in the order named. As a general rule most of the Armenian students in these universities work their way through. A few receive assistance from "home" or from relatives, but ninety per cent of them depend upon their own earnings. They wait on table, clean laboratories, work in kitchens, wash windows, clean house, work in stores and undertake all sorts of jobs. They are a hard working lot of boys and are liked by their fellow students and members of the faculty. Their struggle for an education wins the admiration of all those who come in contact with them. They are successful competitors for scholarships and prizes. As a whole, the Armenian students in our American colleges and universities are a credit to their nation.

NUMBER OF ARMENIAN STUDENTS IN AMERICAN COLLEGES AND UNIVERSITIES IN 1916

1 Academy of Music (N. Y.)	1
2 Albany College	1
3 Amherst College	2
4 Art School (N. Y.)	1
5 Auburn Theological Seminary	1
6 Bible Teachers' School	4
7 Boston University	1
8 Bridgewater Normal School	4
9 Brown University	1
10 Chicago Art Institute	2
11 Chicago Medical School	1
12 Chicago Dental School	3
13 Chicago Musical College	1
14 Chicago University	3
15 College of Pharmacy (Boston)	3
16 College of Physicians and Surgeons	4
17 Columbia University	16
18 Connecticut Nurses' Training School	2
19 Cornell University	4
20 Drexel Institute	1
21 Dewitt Clinton	1
22 Episcopal Theological School	1
23 Hartford Theological Seminary	2
24 Harvard University	14
25 Jefferson Medical	1
26 Lehigh University	1
27 L. A. Normal (Cal.)	2
28 Massachusetts Institute of Technology	12
29 McCormick Theological School	1

30	Michigan University	11
31	Minnesota State College	1
32	Moody Institute	2
33	National University	3
34	Nazarine University	1
35	New England Conservatory of Music	2
36	New Hampshire Agr. College	1
37	New York University	3
38	New York Law School	2
39	Neft College	1
40	Northwestern University	4
41	Oberlin College	1
42	Ohio Northern University	1
43	Ohio State University	9
44	Oklahoma College	1
45	Pacific Medical College	1
46	Philadelphia Dental	1
47	Philadelphia Fine Arts	1
48	Pratt Institute	3
49	Princeton University	1
50	Rensselaer Polytechnic	2
51	Rhode Island College of Pharmacy	1
52	Rhode Island School of Design	1
53	Rutgers College	1
54	Swarthmore College	1
55	Simmons College	1
56	Syracuse University	1
57	Temple College	7
58	Trenton Normal School	1
59	Tufts Dental College	5
60	Union College (Neb.)	1
61	Union Seminary	2
62	Union University	1
63	University of California	22

64 University of Georgia	1
65 University of Illinois	5
66 University of Iowa	1
67 University of Pennsylvania	6
68 University of Vermont	1
69 University of Wisconsin	2
70 Valparaiso University	2
71 Virginia Polytechnic	1
72 Westchester Normal	1
73 Worcester Polytechnic	5
74 Worcester Art School	1
75 Yale University	20
Total	284

The above table was compiled principally from a report of the Armenian Students' Association (1916). Unfortunately the list is not complete. My personal investigation of the number of Armenian students in the public schools, and in Colleges, Universities and other institutions of learning is not, I regret to say, ready for publication at this time. I can state, however, that no other class of immigrants in the United States have taken greater advantage of the educational facilities and opportunities in this country than the Armenians.

Chapter VII

ASSOCIATIONS, PARTIES AND
THE PRESS

THE numerous societies, clubs and associations maintained by
the Armenians in the United States axe, in most instances,
educational and philanthropic. In every colony there is always
some sort of movement to support a school or a hospital back in
the old country. As a general rule immigrants from a certain city
or village in Armenia form a society under the name of their
native town; for example, the Orphans' and Hospital Society of
Sivas, and send the funds derived from initiation fees, annual
dues, donations and gifts to that institution[42]. There are also

---

[42] The following is a partial list of these societies: – The Armenian Library
Union of Fresno, organised in 1897; the Armenian Academy, organised in 1888
but no longer in existence; the Persian Armenian Educational Society, 1010,
New York; Ararat Club, New York, organised in 1890 for military and physical
culture; the Armenian Red Cross Society, New York, 1910; the A. R. F.
Library, New York, 1890; the Armenian Educational Society of Pashaghaggee,
1893, New York; the Educational Society of Hoosemck, 1888, Worcester,
Mass.; the Educational Society of Mornick, 1890, Worcester; the Armenian
Gregorian Educational Society of Hokhe, 1892, Lowell; the Educational Society
of Armenian Gregorians of Dodem, 1891, Providence; Educational Society of
Hasaree Village, 1903, Lawrence Progressive Club of Philadelphia, 1899 (not
affiliated with the Rooseveltian Progressive Party – this is merely a library
club); Educational Society of Arapker, Philadelphia, 1907: Educational Society
of K-Khee Village, 1897, Boston; the Woman's Church Club, 1906. Boston:
Women's Orphan's Society of New Britain, Conn., 1905; the Educational
Society of Pashnashen, 1892, E. Watertown; Educational Society of
Dikranagerd, 1905, Chelsea; Mesrobyan Educational Society of Everigg Village,
1906: Educational Society of Moor Village of 1909. The ArmenoAmerican
Educational Society of Kghi-Khoupsetui; the Armeno- American Educational
Society of Artaghan; the Armeno- American Educational Society of Koshmat;

literary clubs in Boston, Worcester, New York, Providence and Fresno, with libraries containing Armenian books and current literature. The total annual income of all these organizations is placed at seventy-five to one hundred thousand dollars, and practically the whole of this sum is applied directly to the objects intended.

It will serve no practical purpose to give here a detailed account of all the associations that have sprung up from time to time among the Armenian immigrants in America. A brief reference, however, to the work of a few of the most important and active ones will be interesting.

The Armenian Colonial Association of New York City with a branch in Chicago is a very useful institution. It was started in 1909, and a group of well-to-do Armenians pay its entire expenses. The Association renders valuable service to incoming immigrants at Ellis Island, finds employment for those seeking work, gives financial help to those in dire circumstances, and conducts a free public lecture course during the autumn and winter months.

The Armenian Educational Society was founded in 1906 by an Armenian merchant of Chicago in memory of his daughter. It lends money to needy Armenian students taking professional and technical courses in recognized American colleges, theological schools and universities. Its present endowment is $25,000. The annual income from it, together with occasional gifts from various sources and collection of loans, now amounts to about $6,000. On account of a very large demand for assistance this sum is not sufficient to render substantial help to more than a limited few at a time. During the first ten years of service (1901-1916) it

---

the Armeno-American Society of Artaghan; the Armeno-American Educational Society of Ferry. There are also dramatic clubs.

has distributed in form of loans the sum of $18,585.50 to 72 students.

The Armenian Students' Association was formed in 1910, although prior to that many spasmodic attempts were made to bring about a similar society. At the present time the Union has about 250 members. It has a number of commendable aims, such as publishing a good monthly, revising the curriculum of the schools in Armenia, preparing modern textbooks in the Armenian language, and sending properly equipped and educated Armenians to teach school in the old country. As a general rule Armenian students are financially poor and lack of funds has made it impossible for the Union to realize those of its objects that require money.

The United Armenian Societies, organized in 1880 at Constantinople, constitutes one of the foremost educational institutions in Turkey. It establishes and maintains public schools for the Armenians in Armenia and in all parts of the Ottoman Empire. Many of the educational associations in the United States that I have mentioned in a foot-note donate their money to this organization.

The Armenian General Benevolent Union was founded in 1906, at Cairo, Egypt. It has 78 branches in the United States and Canada, 63 in Turkey (before the war), 29 in Europe, 5 in Africa, 3 in India, and 1 in South America, a total of 179 branches with 11,000 active members. "The Society's capital amounts to $253,950 of which sum $156,595 is a statutory fund and is inalienable under the terms of its Constitution; and about $97,355 constitutes a special fund composed of legacies and donations. Since 1906 the total income of the Union derived from the interest on its capital and from special gifts, membership dues and fees amounted to $515,420.

"The funds of the Society are used solely for the benefit of the Armenians in Armenia. This object has been carried out with notable success by founding or endowing schools, hospitals, orphanages and other public institutions; by distributing seeds, cattle and agricultural implements to the peasants; by rendering relief to those who are in distress because of famine, fire or massacre.

"The Union aims to accomplish two objects: one is to bring under one head every Armenian regardless of creed, sex, political belief or place of residence. This is very vital because the Armenians are more or less scattered all over the world and divided among themselves by religious and political differences, and this separation and division of opinion has been their worst enemy. The other aim of the Union is to keep the Armenians in Armenia, conserve what is left of them there, help them to retain title to their native land, and maintain their national integrity. Any one who knows the history of these people, their struggle for existence and their aspirations will at once appreciate the necessity and significance of this great world-wide Association[43]."

The Armenian political parties occupy an important place in the life of these people. It must be understood that these parties have no connection with and take no direct interest whatever in American politics. They are solely concerned with their own national affairs, the main issue of which is the liberation of the Armenian people from the oppression of the Turks and the realization of absolute Independence. There are four of these parties, the Huntchaggist, the Dashnagtzagan, the Reorganized Huntchaggist and the Constitutional Democrats. The Huntchaggist Party is the oldest, having been formed about 1880, or soon after the treaty of Berlin. The Dashnagtzagan Party was established in 1890 by a group of Russian Armenians, and the Reorganized Huntchaggist is an offspring of the old Huntchaggist Party.

---

[43] From a pamphlet prepared by the author for the New York City Branoh of the Union.

As I have stated before, the principal aim of all these parties is one and the same, but their general platforms differ from one another in certain respects. The Dashnagtzagans and the Huntchaggists have socialistic tendencies. The platforms of the others are less radical and tend to follow a moderate course. The total membership of all these parties in the United States is about ten thousand. Each one maintains a newspaper for propaganda work, which I shall take up presently. Each has branches or clubs all over this country. The total amount of money collected from their members in America exceeds $100,000 a year.

The Armenian National Union was created since the commencement of the war at the request of His Excellency Boghos Nubar, the diplomatic representative of his Holiness, the Catholicos, the supreme head of the Armenian Church and the Armenian nation. The headquarters of the Union in the United States is in Boston. It has twenty-one members composed of three delegates each from seven of the largest Armenian organizations, namely the Huntchaggist Party, the Dashnagtzagan Party, the Reorganized Huntchaggist Party, the Constitutional Democrats, the Church of Armenia, the Armenian Evangelical Church and the Armenian General Benevolent Union. The Union has succeeded in bringing about a certain amount of unity among the various Armenian factions; it has become a semi-diplomatic channel through which the claims of the Armenian people have been presented to the Government of the United States; it has done considerable work in setting forth the demands of the Armenians before the American public; it has collected over a million dollars from Armenians in America and has distributed this sum not only to relieve the sufferings of those in distress in Russia, Turkey and Mesopotamia, but also to help the Armenian army that is fighting on the side of the Allies in the Caucasus, in Palestine and Syria.

At the present time there are nineteen newspapers and periodicals published by the Armenians in the United States. Seventeen of these are in the Armenian language and two in English. I mention them in their alphabetical order. Asbarez (The Arena), an organ of the Dashnagtzagan Party, is a weekly published in Fresno, Cal., since 1809. Azk (The Nation) , published in Boston since 1907, is owned by the Constitutional Democratic Party. Bahag (The Sentinel) is the mouthpiece of the Reorganized Huntchaggist Party and is now issued twice a week in Boston. Cilicia, a religious weekly with Armenian characters but in the Turkish language, is printed in New York. Janasser (The Endeavorer) is published by the Armenian Christian Endeavor Union in Fresno. Eritassart Haiasdan (Young Armenia), the chief organ of the Huntchaggist Party, is published in Chicago. Etchmiadzin, another religious monthly allied with the interest of the Armenian Apostolic Church, is printed in Fresno. Gotchnag (The Church Bell), an independent weekly, was originally intended to be the organ of the Protestant Church in America, but it is not a religious paper notwithstanding its name and the fact that its editors have always been ordained ministers. Hairenik (The Fatherland), organized in 1899, is the principal organ of the Dashnagtzagan party and is now published daily in Boston. Housharar, New York, is issued three or four times a year by the central American Committee of the Armenian General Benevolent Union. Nor Ginke (New Life) is another independent weekly issued in Fresno. Punig, a literary monthly, is edited in Boston. Pern, Fresno, is a religious monthly controlled by the Armenian Congregationalists; Sis wan (Fresno) and Taurus (Boston) are independent weeklies. Veradznootun (Renaissance) is a monthly issued in Boston and Yegheghetzi (The Church) is published in New York by the Armenian Evangelical Union. The two periodicals in the English language are, "The Armenian Herald," a well-edited monthly published by the Armenian

National Union, and "The New Armenia" (New York), issued once every two weeks by its editor with the support of subscribers and friends. Both of these periodicals contain good articles on historical and contemporary subjects touching the Armenians, and excellent translation of Armenian stories and poems.

It will be noticed that six of these publications – Asbarez, Etchmiadzin, Jannasser, Nor Ginke, Pern and Siswan are printed in Fresno, California; seven of them – Azk, Bahag, Hairenik, Pnnig, Taurus, Veradznootun and the Armenian Herald are published in Boston. There is one – Eritassart Haiasdan – issued in Chicago, and the remaining six – Celicia, Gotchnag, Housharar, Yegheghetjzi and the New Armenia – are in New York.

The general character and contents of these publications in the Armenian language have something in common. In the first place each is controlled either by a party or a religious organization or a group of individuals. The Asbarez, Azk, Bahag, Veradznootun, Yeritasart Haiasdan and the Hairenik are party papers, financed by their respective organizations and exist primarily for the purpose of promulgating their ideas and maintaining their constituents. The Gotchnag is financed by a few well-to-do business men and merchants. Nor Ginke, Siswan and the Taurus have no organized following, but have some individual supporters. All the others are maintained by various religious organizations. In the second place none of these publications are commercially successful propositions. Not one of them could exist long upon its income from subscribers and advertisements. They have about the same style and contain about the same news and are about the same in standard and quality. The dailies and a few of the weeklies are printed on four to eight large sheets in the manner of American newspapers. Most of the weeklies and monthlies are bound like a small magazine. All the dailies and periodicals contain one or more editorials, articles, letters, foreign and domestic news items, reports from various Armenian settlements, announcements and advertisements[44].

[44] The first periodical or newspaper, in the Armenian language, called Arekag (The Sun) was issued in 1888, in Jersey City, N. J. In 1880 the name of it was changed to Soorhantag and in 1890 it appeared monthly under the name of Azadootun (Freedom) and continued for two years. The next two publications, Ararat, survived two years, and the Haig, appearing off and on for about six years. Yeprad and Dikris came out in 1897: the former was discontinued within a short time, the latter was changed to Tzaiyn-Hairenyatz and became the organ of the old Huntohaggist Party. It ceased in 1907, when there was a rupture between the members of that party. Other weeklies and monthlies such as Loosnag, Shant, Looys, Arak ,Artzive, Zoorna, have appeared from time to time and have been discontinued after a brief existence.

Chapter VIII

CONJUGAL AND LIVING CONDITIONS

THE Immigration Commission has gathered considerable data from 419,347 wage earners relative to their conjugal and living conditions. Six hundred and fifty of those examined were foreign-born Armenians and the statistics compiled upon the information collected shows that 58 per cent of these Armenians were married, 2.2 per cent were widowed and 39.8 per cent were single. Of the married class 49.2 per cent had their wives in the United States and 50.8 per cent in the old country. I believe these figures fairly represent conjugal conditions among the Armenian immigrants, except that the number of the widowed must be larger at the present time. It is interesting to note here the difference between the Armenians and other races with respect to the number having their wives abroad: Among the Armenians it was 50.2 per cent; Bulgarians, 90.0 per cent; Greeks, 74.7 per cent; Macedonians, 96.5 per cent; Roumanians, 73.9 per cent and Servians, 64.5 per cent[45].

As a rule Armenians many in their own race. The ratio among them of female to male immigrants is 1 to 10. Consequently an Armenian girl, regardless of her beauty or station in life, need have no fear of becoming a spinster. Scarcity of suitable girls obliges many a young man to bring over a former sweetheart, or a schoolmate or family acquaintance from the old country. In such cases negotiations are conducted through his and the girl's parents or relatives. This manner of securing a wife, which is prevalent in all European countries, may seem strange to

---

[45] Reports of the Immigration Commission. Abstracts of Reports. Vol. 1, pages 449, 459-460

Americans; but it nevertheless has its advantages. The Armenians handle these matters with the strictest regard for the welfare of the parties concerned and on the highest moral principles. Of course some of these matches prove to be unhappy and sometimes lead to separation and divorce, which is rare among these people; still marriages contracted on the American style do not do away with family troubles.

Inter-marriage with American girls of Irish, Swedish, French, English, Jewish and real Yankee extraction is not uncommon. It occurs more frequently among the educated and long resident Armenians. I am personally acquainted with many of the Armenian lawyers, doctors, dentists, instructors in colleges, engineers, clergymen and pastors, and a great many successful merchants throughout the United States, and I know that more than half of these have American wives. These marriages turn out very happily, judging from what I have actually seen in their homes and from the fact that I have heard of only one divorce in this class. On the other hand intermarriages by the Armenian workmen are not so satisfactory and should be discouraged. Unless a foreigner has acquired a good command of the English language, lived here long enough not only to be able to discriminate between good and bad American girls, but really come to know and understand American ways and habits, he should not attempt to marry other than a girl of his own nationality.

Living conditions among the Armenians in this country do not differ materially from those of Americans, The wealthy and the well-to-do live in the best quarters of the city where they enjoy all the comforts and luxuries that money can provide. Many own their homes. Their children attend the best private schools. Families with moderate incomes also maintain homes in the better sections of the town. The only foreign evidence, perhaps, that one might find in Armenian homes of the rich and well-to-do class is the food, if the wife or the cook is Armenian.

Armenian wage-earners are necessarily compelled to live in the poor sections of our great industrial cities. Immigrants are often blamed for the way they live, but the blame should be placed on the American municipalities which allow the erection of unsanitary tenements and permit the streets to remain congested and dirty. It is a significant fact, however, that Armenian immigrant families of this class have been found to have an average of more rooms per family, to pay more rent and to have less congestion than any of the other newer immigrant races.

The table below, to which I call the reader's special attention, shows the average number of rooms per apartment, the average monthly rent paid for the same, the average number of occupants in each such apartment. A casual study of it will bring out the fact that living conditions among the Armenians are far better than those of a dozen other races which I have chosen at random.

	Average number of rooms per apartment	Average monthly rent paid	Average rent per oapita	Average number of occupants per apartment
Armenians	4.83	11.17	2.25	4.98
Bulgarians	2.41	5.91	.97	6.19
Croatians	4.01	8.55	1.09	7.65
Greeks	4.13	9.02	1.47	6.13
Italians (North)'	3.89	7.66	1.40	5.50
Lithuanians	4.08	8.81	1.47	5.89
Polish	8.82	7.80	1.24	6.06
Russians	3.85	7.46	1.27	5.93
Servians	4.88	9.78	1.08	9.62
Slovaks	8.68	6.84	1.18	5.87

Syrians	4.19	9.80	2.09	4.80

The next table compares old and new immigrant races with respect to congestion. It will be noticed that among the Armenians there is not only less congestion as compared with other new immigrant races, but they are even better than so-called old races.

OLD IMMIGRANTS		NEW IMMIGRANTS	
Number of persons per room	Number of persons per sleeping room	Number of persons per room	Number of persons per sleeping room
Canadian 1.17	2.07	Armenians 1.08	1.97
English .87	1.89	Bulgarians 2.58	3.20
German 1.89	2.15	Greeks 1.48	2.13
Irish 1.02	1.98	Polish 1.58	2.77
Scotch 1.08	2.18	Roumanians 2.57	3.72
		Slovak 1.62	2.66
		Syrians 1.15	1.87

Old and new immigrant races compared with respect to the number of boarders or lodgers for each 100 household[46].

---

[46] Statistics compiled from the Reports of the Immigration Commission. Abstracts of Reports. Vol. 1, pages 420-421, 426, 429, 432.

OLD IMMIGRANTS		NEW IMMIGRANTS	
English	185	Armenians	196
German	816	Bulgarians	829
Irish	169	Croatians	689
		Polish	801
		Roumanians	1228
		Slovak	822
		Syrians	889

The unmarried men and those whose wives are abroad lead the usual bachelor's life. Many who are financially well off live in hotels, others keep apartments and still others find quarters in high-class "furnished" rooms. In smaller communities the well-to-do and educated Armenian boys get in with good American families. The laboring class, especially in our great cities like Boston, Providence, New York and Chicago, settle in the less desirable sections of the town, eat in Armenian restaurants and become habitues of "Oriental cafes," where the evenings are spent in playing backgammon – a game in which Armenians are very proficient – cards and billiards. Armenian leaders often speak disparagingly of these cafes because they are the resort of the idle and the low, still I think they are far better than the bar-rooms. In the small industrial towns like Whitinsville, Mass., where many Armenians are employed, the bachelor class live in groups of twenty, thirty and fifty. A large house is hired, the first floor of which is used as a dining room and cafe and the upper parts for sleeping quarters. An Armenian cook with his helpers prepares the meals and take general care of the premises at a very low cost.

There is practically no charity-seeking among the Armenians. The records of charitable societies in cities like Boston, Worcester, Chicago, Providence, Philadelphia and New York and others show a total average of about 50 a year and these are often taken care of by some individual Armenian or organization. Arrests on criminal charges, especially among the lower classes of unmarried young men, are sometimes made. Judging from my personal experience in courts, I think the number of Armenians arrested for one thing or another is insignificant compared with Italian, Polish, Russian, Greek, Jewish and Syrian immigrants.

The report of the Immigration Commission contain tables regarding 1 the percentage of immigrants owning homes. This investigation appears to have been very limited, but it shows that out of the number from whom data were obtained among the Armenians 8.6 per cent owned their homes; among the Greeks 1.5 per cent; Roumanians, 2.6 per cent; Russians, 1.2 per cent; Syrians, 4.7 per cent. I believe the percentage for the Armenian is too low, particularly in view of the situation in California where seventy-five per cent of the colony, which is the largest in the United States, are owners[47].

The Armenians appear to be one of the foremost races to accept American citizenship. The investigation among immigrant employees in the manufacturing and mining industries shows that over 58 per cent of them are fully naturalized. This is an excellent record when compared with other races, 8 as shown in the following table:

	Per cent.
Armenians	58.2
Bulgarians	.0
Croatians	19.4
Greeks	8.7
Hebrews	24.1
Italians	82.9
Lithuanians	21.9

[47] Reports of the Immigration Commission. Abstracts of Reports, Vol. 1, pages 468 and 487.

Magyar	15.0
Polish	21.6
Portuguese	5.8
Russians	8.8
Ruthenians	14.7
Slovaks	17.1
Syrians	20.0

It must be borne in mind that an Armenian born under the Ottoman flag, when he becomes an American citizen forfeits all his property rights in his native country, and if he ever returns there the United States Government will in no way protect him as an American citizen.

These disadvantages are well known to all Armenians. But I mention them here for the benefit of my readers and to disperse the notion that it is some selfish motive which induces these people to make this change. Armenians who become American citizens do so because they love America, and because they believe it to be not only a duty, but a rare privilege to adopt as their flag the "Stars and Stripes" of this great Commonwealth.

Chapter IX

THE FUTURE

IT is obvious that in the future immigration to the United States will depend to a great extent upon the outcome of the Peace Conference at Paris. Possible legislation by Congress and by the various governments in Europe on this problem will undoubtedly have an important effect on the movement of population from one country to another. It is generally recognized that the world is entering upon a great economic struggle. Enormous national debts must be paid. Oppressed races that have hitherto migrated westward to America in large numbers are to-day facing the dawn of freedom and independence. At the threshold of all these changes it is difficult to say with reasonable certainty what the Armenians will do after the Treaty of Peace is signed.

There are, however, certain eventualities that are apparent. In the first place, the moment all restrictions for traveling are withdrawn a great many Armenians will undoubtedly take immediate advantage of the opportunity and visit their native land to search for their loved ones, to adjust property rights rising from the death of their next of kin, and to acquire first-hand knowledge of conditions there. On the other hand, hundreds of Armenians who have gone through the awful experience of war and deportation are feverishly waiting to leave their devastated homes and seek the United States. Thus for the next few years there will be a constant stream of Armenians either departing from or coming to America.

Just what the Peace Conference will do for Armenia is not known at this writing. If the practical application of the provisions they agree on leaves the country in the hands of a

Power to be exploited by it for its own self-interest, then Armenian immigration to the United States will increase. America has opened the eyes of these people. They know what democracy and independence mean. They are now capable of discerning real freedom by comparison with one that is mortgaged for the benefit of a mortgagee. I do not believe that Armenians who have lived in the United States even for a few years – and ninety-five out of every hundred have been here at least five years because very few have come since the beginning of the war – will ever submit to or be satisfied with conditions which they endured formerly. Those who journey to Armenia after the conclusion of the Treaty of Peace and find that the ultimate independence of their country is as uncertain as in 1878, will at once return to America and their example will be followed by thousands of others.

It is hoped that through the presence and influence of the United States at the Peace Conference, the fate of Armenia will be decided justly and honorably. Armenians demand nothing except what they are entitled to. They ask that the boundaries of their historic kingdom shall be unequivocally defined and settled; that their country be detached completely from Turkey, Russia and Persia; that its independence be declared and a Commission of Englishmen or Americans be appointed to assist in the organization and development of their national institutions. What they want is not sympathy, but liberty. And it is the common expectation of these people all over the world that the United States, England, France and Italy, by virtue of their superior power, will not deprive them of their righteous heritage and the right of self-government.

An independent Armenia will naturally attract many Armenians who are now in the United States. I say naturally because of many considerations. It is impossible to expect a grown-up man who is suddenly transplanted from a far-off country into a shoe factory in Lynn, or a cotton mill in Lawrence, or a slaughter house in Chicago, or a coal mine in Pennsylvania, to blot out from his memory the face of his dear mother, the hills and valleys of his native land and the fond associations of childhood days. As the years go by and he finds himself shackled to hard, humdrum factory life, his longing for the old home becomes stronger. We must recognize, further, that about seventy per cent of the Armenians in the United States are single or widowers or else have their wives on the other side. In other words, they have no home here. Armenian girls are scarce and for most of these men to intermarry with foreigners would be very unwise. But there are hundreds of Armenian orphan girls and widowed women back in Armenia who are absolutely destitute. Who is to take care of them if not the unmarried Armenian men? And if there is security of life and liberty, it would be best, economically and politically, for these people to live in their own native country. Moreover, the Armenians in the United States, farmers, workmen and those engaged in business have saved up some money. These individual savings, however, are too small to undertake enterprises in America, but quite sufficient to be profitably invested in Armenia. We also have hundreds of Armenians in professional life. These lawyers, doctors, dentists, engineers, editors and teachers, all graduates of American colleges and universities, believe that they will have opportunities for service and leadership in Armenia which are denied them in this country. These, I think, are the chief reasons which will influence all classes of Armenians to return to Armenia.

Let us not forget for a moment that should at least two-thirds of the Armenians now in this country – that is about 50,000 of them – go back to Armenia, they would contribute materially to the industrial, political and social reconstruction of their country. The Armenians in America have money. They have acquired skill not only in manufacturing machinery and tools, but in the use of them for productive purpose. With these men in Armenia and with abundance of raw material, the capitalist will encounter no difficulty in securing labor to make machines and in manufacturing shoes, automobiles, silk goods and all sorts of commodities. Also, the Armenians have come in contact with American politics and government. In order to illustrate the lessons they have learned, I might cite here as an example the fact that on February 1, 1919, 25,000 Armenians of voting age, both men and women, throughout the United States chose by ballot patterned after the American system of election, four delegates to the Armenian Congress in Paris. Moreover, the Armenians in America have become accustomed to American habits, and American ways of thought, manner and living. Their association with American

institutions has broadened their vision and outlook, has made them more tolerant and has taught them that it is possible for people differing in color, creed and race, to live together happily. Thus when they go back to Armenia, they will demand American-like homes, American clothing, American railroads, telephones and roads. They will carry with them something of the spirit of America. It is no exaggeration to say that the Armenian immigrants from this country, with the skill, knowledge and experience they have gained here in the sphere of education, industry, government and living conditions, together with the aid of the American missionary forces, and let us hope with the mandate of the United States, will constitute an invaluable asset in the development of the coming Armenian Republic. And they will not only furnish the necessary medium through which American products will find a vast market throughout the East, but will also help to implant and diffuse American ideals and American democracy in that part of the world.

I do not wish to convey the idea that just as soon as an Armenian State or Republic is established every Armenian in the United States will rush over there. Armenians who have married American girls will hesitate long before transferring their families to a foreign country. Children born in the United States of Armenian parents, who go to our public schools, who, unlike other races, attend American churches and associate with American children and who do not read or write Armenian and who constantly use the English language at home, will exert their influence on their parents to persuade them to remain in the United States. There are those, too, who are too old, those who have established business connections and those who are property owners, who will likewise be very slow to take such a step. And those of us who came here in our early youth will find it as hard to go to Armenia as it is for a native-born American to go to China or Brazil. My personal opinion is that if conditions in Armenia are very promising, about two-thirds of the Armenians now in the United States will return to their native country within the next five years. The rest will remain here and their descendants will become absorbed in the great "meltingpot."

www.ingramcontent.com/pod-product-compliance
Lightning Source LLC
Chambersburg PA
CBHW022341280326
41934CB00006B/721